HUCKLEBERRY HANNAH'S

MONTANA COUNTRY SAMPLER

C O O K B O O K

Deanna Hansen-Doying
BLUEBIRD PRESS

Disclaimer: Names of persons and places mentioned in this book are fictitious. Any resemblance to persons, living or dead, mentioned in this book is purely coincidental.

Huckleberry Hannah's Montana Country Sampler
Copyright 1996
by Deanna Hansen-Doying
All rights reserved
second edition (first edition printed first in April 1990 copyright)

ISBN #0-9648099-1-5
Published by Bluebird Press
P.O. Box 664
Eureka, Montana 59917

Manufactured in the United State of America
First Printing April 1996

*This book is dedicated to my husband, Jack, who
tirelessly supports, motivates, and endures me.*

*And to my Lord Jesus Christ, who walks with me
on the good days and carries me through the tough ones.*

<u>With Special Thanks</u>

To my dear friend, Lindalee Mummey, who was truly
there through thick and thin.

The Recipes

This book is designed for anyone who wants to cook great food without the fuss and mess. I think great cooking begins with the simplest ingredients. When I cook, I want to be able to open my cupboard and get the ingredients I need to do the job — I don't want to have to drive 65 miles to get something absurd like pickled hummingbird tongues. And so, this book is for all of you who love to cook, but hate to drive — who love to eat, but hate to spend all day preparing food and then two days cleaning up after yourself.

When I researched this book I made it a point to use only the very best ingredients and so should you. After all, you deserve only the very best. Every recipe is a sure thing, though with a little imagination I know you could make them even better. So get up out of that chair, tuck this book under your arm and march into the kitchen. Let's start creating all the magnificent food you always knew you could. Have a ball! I'll be thinking of you.

P.S. Looking for low-fat substitutions? Any of these recipes can be reduced in fat. Here's an example:

Meg's Super Moist Carrot Cake
Ingredients:
3 cups flour
3 cups sugar
1 tsp. salt
1 Tbl. baking soda
1 Tbl. ground cinnamon
1 tsp. nutmeg
dash ginger
1 1/2 cups corn oil ⟶ change to 1/4 oil and 1 cup applesauce
4 large eggs beaten ⟶ use egg substitute
1 Tbl. vanilla extract
1 tsp. almond extract
1 1/2 cups walnuts ⟶ use 1/2 cup nuts and 1 cup dried fruit
1 1/2 cups coconut ⟶ use 1/2 cup instead
1 1/3 cups carrot puree
3/4 cup crushed pineapple
juice of one lemon

Love,

The Letters

Hannah Marie Markuson, born November 12, 1884, was a young woman, tall and lean with penetrating grey-green eyes flecked with gold, and long abundant chestnut hair. Her features were classic like those found on women painted by 19th century artists; translucent-skinned women with good bones. Her appearance might have been called mysterious, had she not been born in perpetual motion with a manner that was much like a dust storm, and an outrageous laugh that would become her trademark. Nonetheless, she was a beauty in the same way a proud wild pony might be. Hannah believed that everyone should be their own person, and indeed she was. Though Hannah loved adventure, and was hard to tame, she had a reserved conservative side to her that seemed almost introspective — a way about her that suggested she always had a secret. Hannah married Andrew David Hansen, a local rancher, in June 1901 at the age of sixteen and began a new life as a wife and mother.

Emily Jane Bennett, born July 6, 1885, was a little on the fleshy side, though certainly not plump. Perhaps muscular would describe her better. Her small frame and delicate features gave her a near fragile presentation; and good health radiated from her cherub face. She had thick ,wavy, strawberry blond hair, and her eyes were whiskey brown and doe-like. Her nose turned up slightly and was dotted with freckles, which were her bane. Her lips were full, naturally pink, and when she talked her nose moved up and down, ever so slightly, in a charming rather than comical way. Emily liked to laugh and be the center of attention which, of course, was not becoming to a young lady in her day. She was usually the instigator — the one who suggested trouble. In 1901, Emily went away to school in South Carolina. There she met and married Franklin W. Sawyer and became the wife of a clockmaker.

Hannah and Emily grew up together in a small town called Bluebird in Northwestern Montana. Emily might have been the schemer, but Hannah was the planner and the two were a mischievous pair. The girls laughed and played their way through childhood, confided their deepest secrets and most vulnerable feelings through adolescence and shared the tears and joys of adulthood.

In 1901 both young women, separated for what appeared to be forever, began a long distance friendship through letters that lasted over 45 years.

September 8, 1901

Dear Hannah,

    I did not want to write until I was settled a bit and able to collect my thoughts. So much has happened since we said good-bye over a month ago. It seems like forever. Of course, Charleston is lovely, and yes Aunt Beatrice is most accommodating, and yes my head is in a whirl with exciting new things all about me, but I miss you and Montana. Thank goodness Uncle Edward is here with me. He is planning to stay the winter (returning to Montana in May). He will remain, that is, if he and Aunt Beatrice can manage to get along. It is funny to watch them really. I would not call their association adversarial, nor is it friendly. It is not indifferent, nor warm. More like a test of wills and wit, each one trying to get the best of the other. It seems the only time they are completely relaxed in one another's company is over a game of chess. Very odd, don't you think?

    What a grand old home Aunt Beatrice has. Before the Civil War, Heartsong was once a part of an enormous estate. However, most of the property was confiscated and the house nearly destroyed during the war. But now the house and grounds (about 20 acres) have been fully restored. Hannah, it has electric lights and indoor plumbing! Can you imagine?

    The house and its few acres of land sit on a small rise above the water across the harbor from the city. From its verandah I can watch the tide's rise and fall, listen to the gulls calling each other, and smell the salt in the air. Out my bedroom window, I have often watched ships coming and going, to and from the harbor, sailing silently across the horizon. I have grown fond of the sea. How I wish I could share this view with you, Hannah. Knowing how you have longed to see the ocean makes me feel slightly guilty keeping this all to myself, and for this reason I promise to never take it for granted.

2

Soups, Salads & Starters

Though Aunt Beatrice has been very good to me, I soon found out that living in the South requires an entirely different set of manners, let me tell you. Far more formal here, and "proper" is spelled with a capital "P". Gracious sakes! Just how many forks does one need! And the mere thought of wearing my gloves and hat every time I leave the house causes me to sweat (I am supposed to say "perspire" – Aunt Beatrice reminds me that "horses sweat and young ladies perspire"). In addition, Hannah, my vocabulary, I find out is "sadly lacking". I am trying desperately to remember that "yes ma'am" or perhaps "no sir" are the appropriate responses to every question. It is strange indeed that you and I got through our childhood using a simple yes or no, without reprimand or the world coming to an end.

It is very hot here, Hannah. You cannot imagine it. Today I heard Aunt Beatrice's plump Negro housewoman, Belle, whisper to the coachman, Able, that it was hotter than a two peckered owl. I wonder what that means. I will have to remember to ask Aunt Beatrice.

It is the humidity, not the temperature they say is the culprit. The air is heavy and I feel weak with the least exertion. The evenings are not as stifling, however, and we are fortunate that gentle breezes from the sea are the norm. Also, I am told that July and August are the only extraordinarily hot months. I am finding this to be true since September has already proven to be cooler.

I have begun classes at the <u>Academy for Young Ladies Wishing to Someday be Adventurers</u>. Aunt Beatrice would die if she heard me speak of her alma mater in this way! I hate to admit it but I do like it here, and find it interesting. I have met several pleasant young women who have made overtures of friendship. They are, however, so reserved in their manner that I am never sure whether they are being friendly or simply cordial. Not like our friendship, Hannah, which is open and honest and unrestrained. I miss that!

Enough about me for now. Please write and tell me about

Smoked Salmon Mushroom Caps

A perfect starter for any party. Serve them hot!
<u>Makes 18 appetizers</u>

Ingredients:
18 lg. fresh mushrooms
8 oz. cream cheese
2 tbl. mayonnaise
1/4 cup Parmesan cheese
1 tsp. capers
1 tsp. caper juice
4 finely chopped green onions
1/4 lb. smoked salmon
1 tsp. lemon juice

dash each pepper & garlic salt

Utensils:
2 quart mixing bowl
mixer
spatula
cookie sheet
cup of coffee for the cook

Putting it all together:
1. Carefully remove stems from washed and dried mushrooms. Set caps aside and chop stems.
2. Cream together mayonnaise, cream cheese, and caper juice.
3. Add mushroom stems, onions, capers, pepper, and garlic salt. Stir to blend.
4. Crumble smoked salmon and mix with lemon juice. Fold into cream cheese mixture.
5. Stuff caps carefully and place on lightly oiled cookie sheet.
6. Sprinkle caps with a pinch of Parmesan cheese, and broil for 2 minutes or until lightly browned. Serve hot.

Everyone should have a dog and a cat —
a dog to adore them and a cat to ignore them.

Andrew, and the ranch and all you are doing. Do you still like being married? Better yet, does Toulouse?

Dinner is served in five minutes and I must not be late! Belle says, "Hurry up Miss Emily or you for sure get a whoopin". Good-bye, dear Hannah. I will look forward to receiving a letter from you very soon please.

Love, Emily

P.S. Let me quickly say Happy November Birthday, since I am not sure of the post and the time my letters will take to reach you. Let us hope it does not take two months, but I cannot be sure.

Artichoke and Cheese Nibblers

Make these delicious tidbits ahead to save time before a party — They can be reheated in the microwave!

Makes 2 dozen bite sized bits

Ingredients:
2 - 6 oz. jars marinated artichoke hearts
1 small onion finely chopped
1 clove garlic minced
4 eggs beaten
1/4 cup fine dry bread crumbs
1/4 tsp. salt
1/8 tsp. each — pepper, oregano, and tabasco
1/2 lb. sharp cheddar cheese grated
2 Tbl. parsley
1 small jar pimentos (optional)

Utensils:
Mixing bowl
7" X 11" baking dish
frying pan

Putting it all together:

1. Drain liquid from 1 jar artichokes and discard. Drain the liquid from the other jar into frying pan.
2. Add onion and garlic and saute'.
3. Chop artichokes into quarters.
4. Combine with eggs, crumbs, salt, pepper, oregano, and tabasco.
5. Stir in cheese, pimento, and artichokes.
6. Add onion mixture.
7. Pour into buttered baking dish and sprinkle with parsley.
8. Bake at 325 degrees for 30 minutes or until lightly set. Cut into 1" squares. Yum!

*If you are such a good cook,
why do we have to pray before every meal?*

November 18, 1901
Dear Emily,

Andrew sends his best to you along with his hope that you will learn to think before you blab your thoughts to Aunt Beatrice. You always were naive, Emily, but really! Did you think a two peckered owl was perhaps a bird with an extra beak? By now I am sure you will have become educated on the topic!

Life here is wonderful. Andrew and I are very happy, as are Toulouse and Tilly. It took Toulouse a while to learn to live without you and become attached to his new mate, but now they go everywhere together. They swim in the pond and nap in the sun -- true love birds. Toulouse has learned a lesson or two about good manners, however. Neither Meg nor Andrew were about to tolerate his nasty behavior. When Toulouse decided to chase Meg's blue heeler, Doc, with only the worst intentions, Meg really smacked him a good one with the broom. Neither dog, nor gander, nor broom sustained damage, though Toulouse is running a wide berth around Meg!

Well my dear, I have big news. Andrew and I are going to become parents! I had suspected it for a while but now Doctor Torgeson has confirmed that I am pregnant. How can this be? -- Well I know how it can be, but I never dreamed it would be this soon. I am due to deliver this child in March. I was not really surprised at this news -- somehow I sensed it almost immediately. It seems so silly and truly unbelievable that I knew almost at the moment of conception, but truly I did. It was the strangest feeling -- a warmth in my spirit -- like a voice speaking to my heart.

Andrew was thrilled by the news and has been walking about all evening puffed up like a rooster. His mother and I laughed at him. We --Meg and I -- are hoping for a girl. The baby is due in March -- March 20th to be exact, though Meg tells me that babies usually do not care much about schedules and sometimes are tardy little creatures. Andrew

Emily's Shrimp and Crab Dip

Serve this warm in a chafing dish with a variety of
crackers and something cold to drink.

Makes 4 cups

Ingredients:
2 Tbl. chopped green onion
2 Tbl. chopped green pepper
2 Tbl. butter
1 1/4 cup milk
1 cup chopped mushrooms
1/2 cup cream
1 heaping Tbl. cornstarch
2 Tbl. sherry
2 egg yolks
1/8 tsp. nutmeg
1 cup each chopped cooked
shrimp and crab (canned is
o.k.)
1 cup grated cheddar cheese

Utensils:
2 sauce pans
wooden spoons
chafing dish

Putting it all together:

1. Saute' onion and green pepper in butter for 5 minutes. Set aside.
2. In separate sauce pan mix milk, cream, mushrooms, cornstarch, sherry, yolks and nutmeg.
3. Heat slowly, stirring constantly, until mixture begins to thicken.
4. Add onion and green pepper mixture and continue cooking until thick. DO NOT BOIL.
5. Add cheese, shrimp and crab and stir until cheese is melted.
6. Transfer to uncovered chafing dish and keep warm over low.

Remember:
The end doesn't always justify the jeans

wants a boy I know, but he will not say one way or another. Mother Meg tells me privately that she is sure it will be a girl. She claims that she has never been wrong in this department - - that she always guesses correctly. We will see. I feel wonderful - - strong and healthy and not the least bit sick, as I am told others sometimes do. I have a fierce appetite, however, and so I am watching what I eat. I do not want to be the size of Teddy by the time this baby arrives.

You should be glad that you are in Charleston where it is warm, "Miss Emily". Winter came early here like an angry beast. It swooped in on us from the north in a flash and almost caught us unprepared. Thank goodness Meg is such an organized ranch woman. Way back in September she insisted winter was at the door and that we should finish digging all the potatoes and other root crops by October first. She pushed Andrew to get all the firewood cut and stored away by that time as well, and it is a good thing that we listened. We have more than a foot of snow already, and the wind is blowing harshly - - blowing bits of dirt with the snow. Andrew calls it "snirt"!

Your description of the ocean intrigues me. Please tell me more - - I want every detail. Let me taste it, smell it, see it in every detail. Spare nothing! Let me feel like a fish swimming or a ship sailing. Speaking of fish, have you and Uncle Edward done any fishing? Don't spare me those adventures either.

I do not understand your description of Aunt Beatrice and Uncle Edward's relationship. You must tell me more about her, too. Does our dear Uncle Edward find her "attractive"?

I must go. Milking time. I am glad you like school and I do hope you establish some lasting friendship, but just remember where you come from, and do not get too fancy, Missy! Study hard and come home soon. I miss you too!

With love, Hannah

Spicy Cajun Chicken Morsels

This party food can be made in advance and reheated. Serve with a variety of mustards for dipping a plenty of cold drinks.

Serves 8

2 tsp. ground cumin
1/2 tsp. cayenne pepper
dash turmeric
salt to taste
1 1/2 sticks butter
8 skinless boneless chicken breast halves cut into 1 inch pieces

Ingredients:
1 1/2 cups white flour
1 cup finely chopped pecans
1 Tbl. dried oregano
1 tsp. dried thyme

Utensils:
skillet
sauce pan
favorite music to keep the cook company

Putting it all together:
1. Combine the flour, pecans, oregano, cumin, thyme, cayenne, turmeric, and salt in shallow dish.
2. Melt 2/3 of the butter in a small sauce pan (careful not to scorch). Dip each chicken piece first in butter and them in flour mixture. Coat well.
3. Melt remaining butter in a large skillet over medium heat. Add the chicken pieces and saute' until browned on all sides and cooked through. Remove from pan and keep warm.
4. Serve the chicken with toothpicks and your favorite mustard dip.
(I like the following: 2 to 1 hot mustard and honey with a couple drops of sherry.)

One good turn gets all the covers.

Christmas Eve, 1901

Dear Hannah,

A baby! Is it possible? I can certainly imagine you a mother and I am thrilled for you. I must say, though, that I do not envy you. I found out from two of my classmates how babies are reproduced, and worse yet, how they are produced! You should have told me. I felt like such an idiot being the odd person out of that very important conversation. How could I be so ignorant. I am very thrilled about your baby, however, and I too am hoping for a girl. Have you thought of a name. Eleanor might be a nice choice.

My first Christmas away from home has been an odd combination of wonderment and isolation, but I am overwhelmed by the lavishness of the Christmas celebration here. I am like a wide eyed child, and the decorations, lights, and presents are all more than I am accustomed to. And no snow. That is the part that has made me feel lonely for the North and, of course, you. (They say that it does snow here occasionally, but rarely at Christmas.)

Living in the South has caused me to see life in a totally different manner, and my way of thinking has changed. When I was in Montana I happily lived my life from day to day never thinking about the future in the long term sense, or how the world has changed and will change in our lifetime. In contrast to Montana, I suppose the faster pace of city life and the broader culture it represents, has changed me more than I realized. Life moves faster and changes happen more often in the city, and talk of industry, inventions, and transportation is more prevalent. Did you know, Hannah, that they say within our lifetime man will fly? An incredible thought, though two men in North Carolina are building a flying machine at this very moment. If we can fly will we be able to dive deep into the sea, or reach for the stars, as well? You will think I have lost my mind if I continue on this way! Imagine. I

Sweet and Sour Coleslaw

**This unbelieveably easy slaw is
sweet and tart — to tickle your taste buds.**

Ingredients:
2 lbs. green cabbage shredded
1/3 cup seasoned rice vinegar
OR
3 Tbl. sugar and
1/3 cup apple
cider vinegar

1 tsp. salt
1 cup whipping
cream
1/2 cup Best
Foods Mayo
(not salad
dressing)

Utensils:
lg. mixing bowl
chilled serving bowl

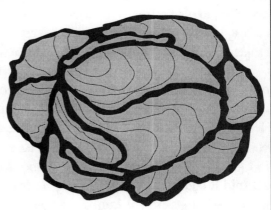

Putting it all together:

1. *Toss all the ingredients together.*
2. *Chill 1 hour.*
3. *Serve.*

*If you want to feel guilty —
just call your mother.*

am even day dreaming in my letters! Aunt Beatrice calls it mental blathering, and it annoys her.

I have met a young man, Hannah. His name is Franklin W. Sawyer and I met him at the Christmas Hop last week. He is twenty, is just finishing his last year at military school and is very intelligent, not to mention charming. Though I do not normally find that a soldier turns my head, I will admit that he is very handsome in his uniform. Franklin's attendance at the Citadel was his Grandfather's dream not his, nor his father's. Though he would make an excellent officer he has chosen civilian life over life in the Army. Franklin is planning to take over his father's business in the near future and not pursue a career of military service. His father is a clockmaker. His work is of the finest craftsmanship, and Franklin feels he is likewise talented.

Let me see, how should I describe Franklin to you. He is tall and lean, with dark hair and blue eyes. He wears spectacles. Do you remember how I always said I disliked the way they look on a man? Well he is very handsome, spectacles or not, and he is a smart dresser. He loves to dance, as I do, and we have the same passion for books and flowers. Unlike me, he thoroughly enjoys horseback riding (I will not hold it against him). Fortunately, he likes to fish and has promised to take me out fishing for large-mouth bass one day. That is all I know about him, except that I am absolutely smitten. He has asked to call on me after Christmas. I am sure Aunt Beatrice will approve of him, but when I told Belle all about him she said, "You keep that young man a guessin' Missy Emily. Don't you be lettin' him get too sure of his self. You in charge child." She treats me like one of her own, (she has five), though she never acts friendly to me unless we are alone. She says Aunt Beatrice would not like it. I am sure that it is part of the lifestyle left over from the days of slavery, and this huge crevasse between negro people and white people is a sad thing indeed. I have grown very fond of Belle and it hurts me to think that her blackness and my whiteness keep us from being friends openly.

I must close for now. Merry Christmas my dear Hannah.
My love to all,
Emily

Crispy Glacier Salad

Tangy and refreshing!
(Eureka French Onion Soup is a perfect compliment.)
<u>Serves 8</u>

<u>Ingredients:</u>
1/2 small onion
1 Tbl. cider vinegar
3 Tbl. spicy brown mustard
1 small egg
1/2 tsp. sugar
salt and pepper to taste
1 cup vegetable oil
1/2 pound bacon fried crisp
2 cups each romaine, red,
butter, and iceberg lettuce torn
into bite-sized pieces
1/2 tsp. lemon juice
1 cup lightly cooked asparagus

spears (cut into 1 inch chunks)
1 cup marinated artichoke
hearts (halved)
5 oz. of blue
cheese

<u>Utensils:</u>
large salad bowl
blender
frying pan

<u>Putting it all together:</u>
1. Fry bacon, drain, and crumble. Set aside to cool.
2. In blender puree the onion with vinegar at low speed.
3. Add lemon juice, sugar, mustard, salt, pepper and
egg. Blend until mixture begins to thicken.
4. Slowly add oil while blender continues to run. When
mixture is thoroughly blended pour into salad bowl.
5. Add vegetables to bowl. Sprinkle with cheese and
toss lightly being careful not
to bruise the lettuce.
6. Serve on chilled plates.

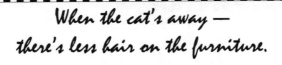

When the cat's away —
there's less hair on the furniture.

February 3, 1902
Dear Emily,

What do you mean about me not telling you. And just who do you think it was that enlightened _me_? Honestly Emily you can be so dim. I did not know much of anything, and what little I did know I guessed. Oh, Aunt Augusta tried to talk about it twice in the last week or so before my wedding, but could only manage a few starts and stops with lots of apron wringing and throat clearing. She made me so uncomfortable that I could not manage to ask a single thing. So there we were. Nothing got said. I got married, and Andrew told me -- or rather showed me -- and really Em, put your fears to rest. You will like it.

Fly indeed! You have lost your mind, not to mention your heart and what I feared most has happened. Franklin W. Sawyer. Tell me more. Smitten? Really. We shall see. Aren't you the girl who said she would never let a man tie her down? Besides you wouldn't dare fall in love with a Southerner and stay down there!

I have sad news, Em. My dear sweet Grandpa passed away quietly in his sleep two weeks ago. He was 87, and I loved him. I wish he had lived to see his first grandchild, but you know he was never the same after Papa died. I will miss him.

I am now in my eighth month and I look remarkably like a walrus. Who would have ever thought that a person's stomach could actually stretch this far. Andrew says I am beautiful, even though he can no longer get his arms around me. I am happy and healthy, and there is a certain feeling about carrying a baby inside you Emily, that cannot be described -- the deepest of love -- a part of me, and a part of Andrew all mixed up together. I am so fortunate to have Mother Meg. I have learned an abundance from her. Thank goodness she is not shy about discussing important topics, in fact, her frankness sometimes causes me to blush. I appreciate her and love her dearly.

Happy Valentines Day next week — Love Hannah

Montana Christmas Salad

A festive center piece for any holiday meal!
Serves 8

Ingredients:
10 cups torn spinach leaves
1 medium-sized avacado,
pitted, peeled, & thinly sliced
Seeds from on pomegranate
1 cup warm seasoned vinegar
dressing (recipe follows)

Seasoned Vinegar Dressing:
1 cup rice vinegar
2 Tbl. honey
1 1/2 Tbl. flour
2 tsp. white wine
1 tsp. Dijon mustard
1 egg beaten
3 Tbl. heavy cream
2 cups extra virgin olive oil
salt and pepper to taste

Make it this way:
1. Combine honey, vinegar,
flour, wine and mustard in
small sauce pan. Heat to
simmering.
2. Over low-heat gradually
whisk in egg, cream, and oil.
3. Season with salt and pepper
to taste.
4. Remove from heat.

Putting it all together:
1. Place spinach in large salad bowl and arrange avacado slices
around edges.
2. Place the pomegranate seeds in the center of the salad.
3. Pour one cup warm dressing over salad, toss at the table, and serve
immediately on salad plates. Delicious!

(Note: Make sure this salad is served as soon as the dressing is
applied. Wilting will occur in a matter of minutes.)

_Any time a child is seen but not heard—
don't wake him._

April 16, 1902

Dear Emily,

She is not a big baby, but what a set of healthy lungs she has. She was born screaming and barely stopped to take a breath for the first two weeks. I am looking forward to her sleeping through the night.

She was born at 8:15 PM on March 31st. We named her Augusta Rose after my Aunt, but Andrew has taken to calling her Babe. He sits with her by the fire in the evening, and rocks for hours. They are a fine picture, Andrew cradling our sleeping baby in one arm while reading a book with his free hand. I knew he would be a good Papa – – as if he had done it all his life.

Babe is beautiful, Emily. She looks just like Andrew and has his blond hair. Unfortunately for all of us, I can tell that her temperament is going to be much like mine – – stubborn, stubborn, stubborn.

The birthing process was not the most pleasant thing I have ever experienced, but no so bad either, Em. I would do it again in the beat of a heart to have my little Augusta Rose. Andrew insisted on bringing Doctor Torgeson here very early on in the labor, but it took five more hours for me to produce that baby. Mother Meg was right there with me and encouraged me through it all. There was a frightening moment, and I began to cry, when we thought the cord was wrapped around the baby's neck. The doctor got very firm with me, almost sharp, and assured me that all was going to be fine. Doctor Torgeson for all his gruff exterior is really nothing but a bowl of mush when it comes to babies. When Augusta was finally delivered, he beamed a broad smile and said, "There then Hannah, just what you hoped for; a beautiful little girl."

When I held her for the first time, Emily, it was if we already knew each other.

Speaking of that little girl, I can hear her loudly reminding me that it is time for dinner. Good-bye for now.

Love, Hannah

Midsummer Potato Salad

Fresh garden herbs, veggies create a confetti of flavors!

Serves 8

Ingredients:

14 new red potatoes cleaned
6 hard-boiled eggs, peeled and halved
1 grated carrot
2 medium scallions or green onions thinly sliced
3 Tbl. fresh dill
2 Tbl. fresh chopped parsley
1 Tbl. caraway seeds
1/2 tsp. salt
1/2 tsp. black pepper
3/4 cup sour cream
3/4 cup Best Foods Mayo
(not salad dressing!)

Utensils:

large pot
large covered bowl

Putting it all together:

1. Place scrubbed potatoes in pot and cover with water. Cook just until tender — 20 to 30 minutes. (Do not over-cook)
2. Combine the eggs, potatoes, carrot, and scallions in a large bowl. Add the dill, parsley, caraway, salt and pepper and toss gently.
3. Mix the sour cream, and mayo and gently fold into potato mixture.
4. Chill thoroughly to blend flavors. Yum!

Body Language:
Where some people have better vocabularies.

May 1, 1905
Dear Emily,

It seems like all Andrew has to do is look at me and I get pregnant! (Meg made a remark about pants hung on the bedpost that made Andrew laugh and me blush.) Yes, we are going to be parents again in late September or early October. I would love to have a little boy, but I have taken on Andrew's attitude and am wishing for health before gender. If it is a girl we will name her Elizabeth Anne Marie; if a boy Andrew David Jr. -- Beth or A.J. for short.

That is the only good news I have to report; the rest sickens me. Abby met a man last year at the county fair. Tom Wheeler said he was an "actor", and was only working as a carnival hand -- temporarily between "theatre engagements". Abby was only fifteen then, and so impressionable. He must have been at least thirty! Abby fell blindly in love, and she wrote to him often at an address he had given her in Kansas City. I was relieved when he did not write in return, but then he came back unexpectedly last week. He said he was traveling through to Alaska. Yesterday, Abby secretly ran off with him. She left a note for Aunt Augusta with the hope that we all would forgive her -- that we would love her in spite of an irresistible urge to follow Tom Wheeler and the life of travel and adventure that he promised. Emily, when I read that note I recognized Laurel at once. I realized, with a knot in my stomach, that though I had inherited our mother's features, Abby had inherited her nature. I have had a sleepless night. I sat by the fire and pondered Abby's fate. If I had shown Laurel's letters to Abby -- mine as well as hers -- could I have spared Abby the life she will surely have? Should I have talked to her about Laurel? I certainly would have if she had asked me -- if she had been the least bit curious I would have shared it all with her. I am tortured by regrets and now I don't know where Abby is. Uncle Justin has hired someone to find her but the only thing we know is that she "may" have gone north.

I wish you were here. Pray for us, Em.
Love Hannah

Best Caesar Salad

**This is the most delicious Caesar you will ever taste.
(even Caesar agrees!)**

4 large portions

Ingredients:

1 lg. head romaine lettuce
2 cloves garlic crushed
1 diced green onion
1/2 cup olive or peanut oil
1 raw egg slightly beaten
3 Tbl. fresh lemon juice
3 anchovies drained, chopped
2 hard-boiled eggs, quartered
1/2 cup freshly grated
Parmesan cheese
3/4 cup croutons (rye, wheat
pumpernickel, whatever.)
freshly ground pepper to taste

Utensils:

large salad bowl
chilled dinner plates

Putting it all together:

1. Clean, dry, and chill romaine. Tear leaves into large pieces.
2. Whisk raw egg, garlic, onion, lemon juice, and oil in salad bowl.
3. Add the lettuce, anchovies and hard-boiled eggs, and toss lightly.
4. Sprinkle with cheese, pepper and croutons and serve immediately.

Banker: A person who lends you his umbrella on a sunny day, then takes it back the minute it rains.

May 12, 1905
My dearest Hannah,

I promised to write just as soon as we were settled into our new home. And though we are just barely that, I could not wait to send you a complete accounting of our new home here on the Ashley River. Hannah, it is simply the loveliest house! Franklin must have driven himself mad looking for just the perfect residence. I will not bore you with all the details, but I will tell you that we have a beautiful verandah complete with a swing! It is just like the one you and I used to spend summer afternoons in when we were girls. I am sure Franklin had it installed especially for me so I would not feel so homesick. All Franklin's family has been so very kind and helpful; truly making every effort to make me feel at home and to help me adjust. I use the term "all family" loosely, since Franklin's eldest sister, Leona is just as nasty to me as ever. What I ever did to deserve her, I will never know. God loves her too, I guess. Give me strength!

I do miss Montana so! Make no mistake, I am thrilled to live in such a beautiful city as Charleston, but just the same, change is never easy. Especially for someone like me. I'm sure I will grow to love it here, though Montana will always be my home, and you my dearest friend.

Franklin's business is located very near to the college where we met. I can hardly believe that it was almost five years ago. I was such a child then. I can still remember how self-conscious I was when I was near him. Imagine anyone ever being nervous around that sweet gentle soul, but everything seemed to embarrass me then. I suppose I have not changed all that much. After all, I will be 20 in July and you would think I would out-grow all that nonsense and be more sophisticated. Anyway, I am off the subject. What I meant to say before I started prattling, was that Franklin's shop is just wonderful and perfect for a clockmaker. It's not as big as his father's shop was, but perfect nonetheless. Franklin is so very talented, and I am positive he will be a huge success.

Mother is coming for a visit and will arrive tomorrow. She says

1920 Waldorf Salad

The way it used to be.

Serves 8

Ingredients:

2 cups miniature marshmallows
4 cups seedless green grapes
3 cups unpeeled chopped tart red apples
1 peeled orange
1/4 cup pineapple juice

1/2 cup chopped celery
1/2 cup chopped walnuts or pecans
1/2 cup seedless raisins or coarse chopped dates
1 cup whipping cream
1/2 cup mayonnaise
1 Tbl. sugar

Utensils:

large chilled bowl
large chilled plates
a kiss for the cook

Putting it all together:

1. Toss together first five ingredients. Then add celery, nuts, and raisins.
2. Whip cream with sugar and stir in mayonnaise.
3. Toss everything together.
4. Chill and serve. Yikes is this good!

_When a man brings home flowers
for no reason — there's a reason._

she is coming to help me "get settled". I can hardly wait. (misery)

Here I have been going on about me and have not bothered to thank you for the wonderful quilt you made us for our wedding present. Hannah, you simply amaze me! Just when I think you are the biggest oaf of a girl, you surprise me with an intricate piece of work like this. The Prussian blue in the quilt matches exactly the flowered print of my bedroom draperies. Thank you, dear. I will cherish it forever. As a matter of fact, I have been spending a considerable amount of afternoon time "under" it recently. I simply do not seem to have a lot of energy as of late. Probably just the change in climate.

Missing you.
Emily Bennett Sawyer

P.S. I just this moment received your letter. I am both shocked by the news of Abby and happy about your coming baby. Surely Abby will come to her senses and be home before we know it. Please know that I am with you in spirit.

All my love, Em

Sunday Supper Soup

This hearty soup is a meal in itself but you might consider serving it with sourdough bread and a tossed salad.
Serves 8

Ingredients:

1 lbs. extra lean ground beef
2 eggs slightly beaten
1/2 cup bread crumbs
1 Tbl. parsley
2 cloves crushed garlic
milk to moisten
1/4 cup olive oil
1 lg. onion chopped
1/2 cup diced celery
1 tsp. oregano
1/2 tsp. basil
1 Tbl garlic powder
2 bay leaves

3 Tbl. flour
salt and pepper to taste
2 cups sliced carrots
6 beef bouillon cubes
1 lg. can stewed tomatoes
mashed
3 cups water
1 cup white wine
1 cup Parmesan

Utensils:

lg. soup pot
8 hungry people

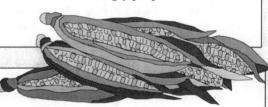

Putting it all together:

1. In lg. bowl combine first six ingredients and add a pinch of salt and pepper. Mix well. (Get your hands into it). Make small meatballs.
2. In soup pot, brown meatballs in olive oil. Then remove meat from pot and set aside.
3. In pot: add onions and celery and saute' until onions are clear.
4. Add remaining ingredients (except carrots and cheese) to pot and simmer 30 minutes to blend spices. Salt and pepper to taste.
5. Add the meatballs and carrots and simmer until carrots are tender.
6. Remove bay leaves.
7. Stir in cheese and serve hot in soup plates if you have them.

Deep Breathing adds to your longevity — especially if you can do it for 90 years or more.

August 17, 1905
Dear Emily,

So you are finally pregnant!
I know you hate that word, but
pregnant is exactly what you are and
saying you are "expecting" is a bit silly,
don't you think? Expecting what? That it will snow --
that the mail will arrive by one o'clock -- WHAT?
Honestly, Emily, sometimes you are just plain dim. I am
so glad that I live on a ranch where life is just life. Well
I certainly did not mean to write and throttle you. Sorry, I
am just so "expecting" myself and it is so hot this year that I
suppose my nerves are a bit frayed. At any rate, you are
going to be a mother in December, and I am thrilled for you,
Em. After all, I must thoroughly believe in motherhood
since I nearly have three of my own. (As you often remind
me; three in five years!) I just do not know what happened
-- well I do, but explaining it would really make your lip
twitch. I guess I am simply meant to have lots of
youngsters around.

I got a letter from Abby last week and she is
"expecting" too. She wrote that her baby is due in early
April, and she claims she is very happy with Tom, though I
am still pessimistic. I am grateful, however, that she has
kept in touch with us. As you recall it was a long two
months before we heard a word from her. She says nothing
of her life there in Alaska, and I am very worried, but she
has to live her own life and I have to love her inspite of what
I consider poor decisions on her part.

It looks like the two of you are in the same boat, you
might say. I am glad it is you and Abby -- and soon no
longer me. No more babies for me! I am not yet twenty-one
and it seems as though I have been "expecting" forever. I
feel like my maternity clothes should be called eternity
clothes. You realize that Babe is three, and Mary Ella just

Chunky Clam Chowder

An all time favorite — Thick creamy and fillling!
<u>Serves 8</u>

<u>*Ingredients:*</u>
1/4 pound bacon
1 small diced onion
1 clove garlic crushed
1/2 green pepper diced
2 stalks celery diced
2 - 10 oz. cans clams
(save liquid!)
1 cup water
2 cups diced potatoes (raw)
1 cup diced carrots

1 tsp. worcestershire sauce
1/4 tsp. salt
dash pepper
1 cup milk
1 cup cream
1 bay leaf

<u>*Utensils:*</u>
lg. soup pot
frying pan
1 really cold day

<u>*Putting it all together:*</u>

1. Saute' bacon, onion, garlic, celery and green pepper for 5 minutes. Transfer to soup pot.
2. Add bay leaf, liquid from clams, water, diced potatoes, carrots, salt and pepper.
3. Simmer until potatoes and carrots are barely tender.
4. Add worcestershire sauce, clams, milk and cream.
5. Heat to simmer. DO NOT BOIL!
6. Remove bay leaf. Serve hot.

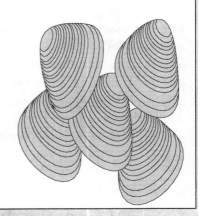

Husbands are those wonderful creatures with "selective hearing" and "convenient amnesia"

turned two, and in less than two months I will have another? Andrew loves having babies around, as do I, but enough! The ranch alone represents more work than I can accomplish. Andrew agrees with me, but I know in his heart that he wishes he had a son and it makes me feel so guilty.

What happened to our childhood, Emily, and all the fun we had together? I suppose I never imagined that we would ever be separated, and now you are so far away. I feel absolutely amputated. Am I ever going to see you again? And what is this "Emily Bennett Sawyer" business? How smug. You with your lovely musical name and me stuck with "Hannah Hansen". It almost sounds like the squeak and hiss of a broken wheel. I could have kept my maiden name, too, you know. But Hannah Markuson Hansen would really have been a handle. I suppose I should leave the fancy names to fancy ladies like you.

What a good summer we are having despite the recent hot spell. Andrew took all his girls for a picnic and some fishing down by Sutter's Pond after church last Sunday. Pastor Burkey's "stop to smell the roses sermon" must have gotten to him. At any rate, we all had a wonderful time. All except Mary Ella, that is. Babe pushed her into the water, of course. I do not understand where a beautiful little girl like Babe got such a nasty streak! She is always picking on somebody. I just know the Lord gave her to me to teach me patience.

Goodbye for now, sweet Emily. My love to Franklin and his family - - even Leona.

Love, Hannah

Eureka! Onion Soup

Delightful, subtle flavors to savor.
<u>Serves 8</u>

Ingredients:
1/4 cup olive oil
4 large onions thinly sliced
4 cloves garlic crushed
1 tsp. sugar
1/2 cup flour
10 cups beef stock (cool)
1 cup white wine
2 tsp. worcestershire sauce
1 tsp. parsley
1/4 tsp. sage
1/4 tsp. thyme
1/4 tsp. coriander
1/4 tsp. allspice
1/2 lb. sliced Swiss cheese
2 cups croutons

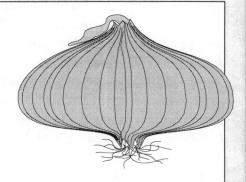

Utensils:
large soup pot
soup crocks

Putting it all together:

1. In soup pot, saute' onions and garlic in olive oil.
2. Whisk flour into beef stock and add to pot. Stir to simmer.
3. Add remaining ingredients (except cheese and croutons).
4. Simmer 30 minutes longer.
5. Ladle into soup crocks. Lay a slice of Swiss on top of each individual soup and broil to melt.
6. Sprinkle with croutons. Serve hot.

*Advice to wives: Do all the talking yourselves.
It saves time and prevents arguments.*

January 5, 1906

Dear Hannah,

She is a little dark haired blue eyed angel. Or at least that is how Franklin describes her to everyone who will listen. She was born December 30th just before midnight in a very easy birth. Honestly, Franklin's family had filled me with such horror stories that I was truly terrified, but all went remarkably well. We named her Julianna Leona. Julianna after Franklin's grandmother, which pleases me since Grandma Sawyer is such a dear old soul. And Leona after you know who. I was going to protest but discretion is the better part of valor you understand.

Julianna is the best baby, Hannah, and so beautiful. She does not look anything like my side of the family, thank goodness. I was so afraid that she would inherit the Bennett strawberry hair! I am hoping she will have my green eyes though, and I am just vain enough to be ungraciously proud. Now I can understand that special love you have for your babies, Hannah. It is indeed unimaginable. To think that tiny Julianna is a part of me, that she grew inside me for all those months and now she is here with me. I am amazed every day at how she responds to my touch and listens to my voice. It is not within my vocabulary to describe.

Speaking of being proud. Franklin is the worst. He cannot keep his hands off her, and carries her with him everywhere when he is at home. He holds her by the hour in the rocker next to the fire, whistling away while he rocks. I am sure you well remember me mentioning Franklin's off key whistle. I am frightened to death he will make her tone deaf, but I think she understands him better than anyone. She simply smiles and gurgles in spite of that annoying noise he makes. It amazes me that a man who has such a superb singing voice, was cursed with a whistle that is reminiscent of fingernails grating on a blackboard.

No other big news to report. I will write again soon. Hug all your brood especially that little one.

Love, Emily

Hannah's Garden Tomato Soup

Lovely, this one! Hearty, but not heavy.
<u>Serves 8</u>

<u>Ingredients:</u>
2 leeks (whites only) diced
1/4 cup olive oil
2 carrots diced
1 small parsnip diced
3 cloves garlic crushed
1 lg. potato diced
1/3 cup red wine
2 lg. cans stewed tomatoes
mashed
10 cups beef stock
1 Tbl. parsley
2 Tbl. basil
3 tsp. tarragon
1/2 tsp. nutmeg
salt and pepper to taste

<u>Utensils:</u>
lg. soup pot
cup of hot Earl Grey tea for
the cook

<u>Putting it all together:</u>

1. In soup pot, saute' first six ingredients for 5 minutes.
2. Add beef stock and wine. Simmer ten minutes.
3. Add tomatoes and spices. Simmer 15 minutes covered and 30 minutes longer, uncovered.
4. Serve hot with biscuits and honey.

Three rules for healthy teeth: Brush after every meal, see your dentist twice a year, and mind your own business.

September 12, 1906
Dear Emily,

          The most horrible thing has happened and though my life has not been without loss this loss is too great.

          I had not heard from Abby in sometime and found this strange but thought she must be so busy with her babies that she, understandably, had not had time to write. You remember Tom Wheeler, my sister's husband? He arrived today, along with a disreputable looking woman he called Cora, and my two baby nieces - - Abby's twins.

          I was trimming the roses in the front of the house when they drove up in a buggy that was as weather beaten as its passengers. The sight of him with that woman made my blood run cold and as I rushed toward the gate my heart knew something had happened to Abby. Though my mind told me to run the other way and not listen to what Tom Wheeler had to say, I flung the gate open and stood there waiting for him to speak; glaring at him, afraid to ask where Abby was.

          He said, "I am very sorry ma'am, but your sister died a month ago. Appendicitis took her. I cannot care for these girls and am hoping to leave them here with you." Emily, I just stood there while grief and disbelief washed its nauseating cold over me. Then he got out of the buggy, and without another word set the babies, sleeping in their baskets, on the ground at my feet. He drove away without ever looking back, Em. What a miserable man. I hope that Ruth and Clare will never be unfortunate enough to meet him.

          Tonight, I took the letter Laurel had left for Abby out of my hope chest, and burned it without looking at its contents. How could I read it? And what difference would it make? My sister is gone and I do not know where she is buried, or what has truly happened to her. It is all too tragic to be believed. I am tortured by regrets. I feel inconsolable.

Love Hannah

32

Market Day Lentil Soup

**This a real winner. Gently spicy and an aroma
that will draw you into the kitchen!**
<u>Serves 6</u>

<u>Ingredients:</u>
3/4 cup onion chopped
3/4 cup celery chopped
1/2 cup carrots diced
1 clove garlic crushed
2 Tbl. olive oil
6 cups chicken stock
1 lg. can stewed tomatoes
3/4 cup lentils
3/4 cup barley
1/2 tsp. oregano

1/2 tsp. pepper
1/4 tsp. turmeric powder
1/4 tsp. curry powder
1/4 tsp salt

<u>Utensils:</u>
lg. stock pot

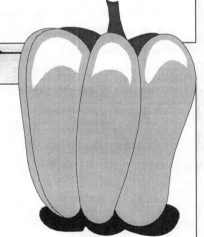

<u>Putting it all together:</u>

1. In stock pot, saute' first five
ingredients.
2. Add chicken stock, tomatoes,
lentils, barley, and spices.
3. Simmer 1 hour. Serve hot.

*A kiss is a pleasant reminder
that two heads are better than one.*

October 15, 1906

Dear Hannah,

Oh, how I wish I could be there to comfort you. I wept all day over your letter. I cannot begin to tell you how sorry I am about Abby. What a terrible tragedy! How could something like this happen? And with Ruth and Clare only four months old! Hannah, I know those babies will be a joy to you even though the loss of your sister is still so fresh. In the meantime, shower those little girls with all the love you possibly can. You are a strong girl, Hannah. I know you can get through all this. Everything has its purpose and though all is black around you now, this pain will pass. Surround yourself with all the good memories of Abby. Remember her for those precious little girls. There will be so much they will want to know someday. Why am I so far away when you need me the most! Is there anything I can do? You will be in my prayers every day, my dear, and even though I am far away, God is right beside you.

All my love, Emily

Broccoli Cheese Soup

Rich and Creamy — a soup to chew!
<u>Serves 4</u>

<u>*Ingredients:*</u>
3/4 cup onion
2 Tbl. olive oil
3 cups chicken stock
1/2 cup chopped broccoli
1/2 cup cauliflower
1/2 tsp. garlic powder
1/2 tsp. salt

dash pepper
1/2 lb. grated sharp cheddar
cheese
3 cups milk
1 cup cream

<u>*Utensils:*</u>
 lg. stock pot

<u>*Putting it all together:*</u>

1. Steam cauliflower and broccoli and set aside.
2. In stock pot, saute' onion in oil until clear.
3. Add veggies and spices to pot.
4. Add milk, cream and cheese and stir.
5. Heat to melt cheese, but DO NOT BOIL.
6. Serve hot in soup plates.

I think age is a high price to pay for maturity.

August 10, 1909
Dear Em,

      The girls are finally in bed, and Andrew is still using the last available daylight to finish repairing the wagon that broke in the midst of haying today. Aggravation seems to be his companion during harvest time. Meg has gone on to bed. She is not the night owl she used to be. After all, she will be 70 in June.

      All is well here, though over the past three years there were times when I did not believe that life would ever be normal again. Abby's death shook me to my very foundation. It was just so unexpected. Andrew was strong for both of us -- you know how he is -- he never says much, but he is as constant as the seasons. And how wonderful you have been. Your prayers and letters have sustained me, Emily.

      Aunt Augusta and Uncle Justin have decided to move to Missoula and will be leaving in less than two weeks. Uncle Justin has purchased a newspaper there, and since Grandfather passed away , they felt no need to stay -- free to move on. This morning over breakfast, Andrew and I realized that I have no more family. Aunt Augusta and Uncle Justin were the last. I do not mean to speak of them as if they were deceased, but Missoula is a quite a distance and I imagine our visits will be few. When are we going to be able to fly, Emily?!

      Life has settled into a comfortable routine and everyone is happy. Ruth and Clare are indeed a joy. I love them as much as I do my own girls. As a matter of fact, I cannot imagine life without them now, and neither can Andrew. Poor Andrew! Life with 6 females cannot be easy, but he takes everything in stride even when all the children are so different from each other.

      Ruth and Clare have absolutely nothing in common. Surprising I know, but honestly Emily, they do not look like they could be sisters let alone twins. In addition, their personalities are like night and day. Clare is small and dark and painfully shy, but she is easy to love, and is always trying to please. Ruth, on the other hand, is blond and full of energy. She is into everything

Breads & Pastries

and is an incredible dare-devil. Yesterday, I found her in the horse corral! Be still my heart! Thank God big animals understand little children.

As for the other three. Babe is as pretty as ever, with an eye for expensive everything. Ranch life is definitely beneath this one. She still fights with all her sisters, but she is a good friend to me. Mary Ella is my studious one. Books and school are the center of her world — a deep thinker like her father. Beth thinks life inside the house is a bore, and that she should become a permanent outdoor fixture. Animals and flowers and birds and sunsets are the only things important to her. It really is funny. They are all so different, but I love them all the same.

There are a few things that we all like to do together. Sunday afternoons at Perry Creek picking huckleberries is certainly one of them. All of us laughing and foraging around in those bushes reminded me of you and I doing the same when we were twelve. The memory gave me a moment of panic, thinking of that bear standing up right in front of us. I screamed. You took one look at that bear and did not know whether to run or faint. The look on your face, Emily, still makes me laugh. You decided running was the better course of action, and once you started you absolutely would not stop. The bear was just as scared, and running faster than you were, but in the opposite direction, though you were positive he was right on your heels. I bet you are still afraid of bears. Actually I think of you more often when I am making huckleberry pies than I do when I am picking berries. You really loved huckleberry pie. Remember when your mother was determined that you were going to learn to make pies and she tried and tried to teach you? She nearly had to drag you into the kitchen by your ankles and, in the end, you out-witted her. You paid Becky Parsons to make a pie for you and you gave it to your mother as a perfect display of your work! You imp. I wonder if she ever knew.

I can see Andrew coming from the barn and I am sure he is tired and hungry. Will close for now. Love to Franklin and Julianna. Congratulations on your wonderful news! It's up to you now. This one just has to be a boy! Love Hannah

Hannah's Sunbeam Bread

Light, semi-sweet and moist.
Makes two large loaves or 2 doz. rolls.

Ingredients:
2 Tbl dry yeast
1/4 cup <u>lukewarm</u> water
1/2 tsp. sugar
Dissolve sugar and yeast in water and set aside.

1/3 cup sugar
1 cup powdered milk (dry)
2 cups warm water
1/2 cup butter-flavored shortening
1 tsp. salt

3 eggs slightly beaten
4-5 cups flour
butter for basting

Utensils:
cookie sheet or 2 lg. bread pans
lg. mixing bowl
mixer

Putting it all together:
1. Combine shortening, water, milk, sugar, and salt in mixing bowl. Mix at low speed to dissolve.
2. Add eggs. Mix in thoroughly.
3. Add 2 cups flour and yeast mixture. Mix lightly.
4. Remove from mixer and turn dough out onto floured board. Mixture may be loose.
5. Knead in remaining flour or until dough is firm but not dry.
6. Place dough in clean oiled bowl. Cover and place in warm breeze-free spot to rise.
7. When twice its original size, turn out onto floured board and form into loaves or rolls.
8. Let rise again. Then bake at 350 degrees for 20-30 minutes or until golden. Do not over bake.
9. Serve warm from the oven.

Don't treat your body like you have a spare in the trunk.

October 3, 1909
Dear Hannah,
       Franklin's two maiden aunts have been here visiting with us for the past two weeks. I am guessing Olivia and Lily are in their mid to late sixties.

    Olivia is the elder of the two, and is very hard of hearing. (Unless you whisper something near her, whereupon, her hearing becomes instantly acute.) She is a large woman and tends to doze off often (sometimes in the middle of a sentence). Lily, on the other hand, is far less lethargic, but has a mind that can best be described as misplaced. She insists on calling me Edna. Darlings, both of them really, but what characters they are; two sisters that have grown old and into extreme eccentricity together.

    We were sitting on the verandah last evening and Franklin, thinking they would find it interesting, asked me to tell the sisters a little about Montana. I did so, and when I was finished Lily said, "Oh, that was very nice, Edna." Now please understand Hannah, it had been the fifth time that day Lily had called me Edna, and to be honest I was beginning to get a wee bit agitated.

    I decided to venture a query; to ask her why indeed she continued to call me by that name. I said to her," Lily dear, why is it you insist on calling me, Edna? Do I look like someone you once knew by that name? Are my mannerisms similar or does my voice remind you of another person?"

    She turned to me soberly, and with a quizzical expression said. "Well no, dear. You are the only Edna I know."

    Franklin nearly convulsed in his attempts to get control of his laughter, while I tried to respond appropriately. I settled for, "Yes ma'am.". Irritating. Let me change the subject.

    Julianna is growing and is such a pleasant child. She

Old-Fashioned Sourdough Bread

Don't try this when you're in a hurry.
It takes time but, oh is it worth it!
<u>Makes 3 - 4 small loaves</u>

Starter is made and kept forever or until you choose not have it any more. You simply replenish the starter every time you make bread. I actually know people who have starter that is over 20 years old! Ready? Let's make sourdough.

The starter:
2 cups flour
1/2 tsp. dry yeast
3 Tbl. sugar
2 cups warm water
1 tsp. salt

In a 2 quart crock, stir all ingredients together to make a smooth paste. Cover and set in a warm place to "sour". Stir several times a day for 3 days. At the end of the third day, place mixture in refrigerator. The day before you make bread, follow the directions for **"the night before"**.

"The night before": (thought I was kidding, didn't you?)
2 cups warm water
1 tsp. sugar
1/2 tsp. salt
2 cups flour
(continued next page)

The best way to remember your
wife's birthday is to forget it once!

41

has become the apple of her Grandmother and Grandfather Sawyer's eyes and I am often afraid they will spoil her, but Julianna does not seem to be affected by gifts and attention. She seems strangely secure, and wise beyond her years. Deep water would describe her. You would not think I was talking about a five year old. Yesterday, a neighbor girl brought over her new game of checkers to show Julianna (a game Julianna had never played). Later I peeked out the window and found them playing the game out on the veranda. I heard the neighbor girl tell Julianna quite sharply that she was playing the game incorrectly. Julianna replied," Well, it is hard to play the game if you do not know the rules, Rachel." How true about many things, was my private thought.

I stopped by to see Aunt Beatrice today and caught her with a letter from Uncle Edward. I wonder what is really going on between those two. But try as I might I can't get any information out of either one of them. Uncle Edward is coming here soon to see the baby and I will try to wriggle the truth out of him. Curiosity is killing me.

Franklin and I have been out fly fishing again today. Nowadays, I can assure you, that if the fish are biting anywhere within a 15 mile radius, Franklin cannot be found at home. He has gotten extremely proficient, Hannah, and I am getting very tried of eating fish!

Love, Emily

Add all the ingredients to your starter mix and stir vigorously until smooth. Let stand at room temperature overnight. Then next morning, put 2 cups of this mixture back into the refrigerator to preserve starter for the next time.

Making the Bread: (Whew! Finally.)

2 cups starter
1 tsp. salt
2 cups warm water
3 Tbl. olive oil
1/2 cup sugar
6 - 8 cups flour
1 egg beaten with 2 Tbl. milk

1. Combine starter, salt, warm water, oil, sugar and 2 cups flour together in large bowl.
2. Stir to blend.
3. Add flour to make managable dough.
4. Turn out onto floured board.
5. Knead in remaining flour or until dough is firm but not dry.
6. Place dough in clean oiled bowl. Cover and place in warm breeze-free spot to rise.
7. When twice its original size, turn out onto floured board and form into loaves or rolls.
8. Let rise again. Then bake at 350 degrees for 20-30 minutes or until golden. Do not over bake.
9. Baste with egg mixture while still hot. This gives bread a thick "crusty" crust.
10. Serve warm from the oven.
11. Eat until you can't stand up.

May your life be like a roll of toilet paper —long and useful.

February 28, 1910
Dear Hannah,

Amanda Bennett Sawyer is a very appropriate name for our new baby girl, since she is a Bennett through and through.

Strawberry blond hair, and a personality to match. She has a temper to go with all her curly red hair, and I believe I have seen but a preview of the interesting life I will lead as the mother of this child. Franklin calls her his feisty female, and is far more patient with her than I. Nonetheless, Amanda is a beautiful baby, and though strong-willed, I love her dearly. She was born on the 2nd of this month, and the birth was extremely difficult. (Why does this not surprise me?) Though Amanda was not a very big baby, she was born in the breech position, and that caused several unpleasant complications. There was the odd moment that I was frightened, Hannah, but as you can see we both survived. When I think of you birthing babies at home rather than in the safety of a hospital, my spine suffers a chill. I do realize that babies have been born outside the security of hospitals for all of history, but I am happy they were not mine! I will leave that to sturdier women like you.

Julianna simply adores her new sister and is more than anxious to hold and care for Amanda. Julianna is not the least bit bothered by her sister's temperament, and spends hours with her every day. Amanda wails, and Julianna consoles her. My two girls. One so placid, like the sea on a calm day, and the other like a raging forest fire. What was God thinking of? All our love from our brood to yours.
Love, Emily,

P.S. Franklin reminds me to tell Andrew that he caught a six pound bass last Sunday afternoon, out at the lake, and he dares Andrew to beat that weight before the summer is through. Oh, dear. Another contest of skill between these men of ours. As you remember, Hannah, the last fishing challenge had to do with length and I have yet to decide which one of them was the bigger liar!

Oatmeal Ranch Bread

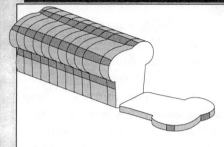

This full bodied bread is great with soup!

Makes 2 large loaves

1/4 cup brown sugar
1/2 cup vegetable oil
1 tsp. salt
3 eggs beaten
4-5 cups white flour
1 cup whole wheat flour (fine ground)

Ingredients:
2 Tbl. dry yeast
1/4 cup <u>lukewarm</u> water
1/2 tsp. sugar
Dissolve sugar and yeast in water and set aside.
2 cups boiling water
1 1/4 cups quick oats
1/2 cup molasses

Utensils:
2 large loaf pans
large mixing bowl
mixer

Putting it all together:
1. Combine 2 cups water & oats in mixing bowl and soak 30 minutes.
2. With mixer, blend into oat mixture, brown sugar, molasses, oil, salt, and eggs
3. Add whole wheat flour and yeast mixture. Mix lightly.
4. Remove from mixer and turn dough out onto floured board. Mixture may be loose.
5. Knead in remaining flour or until dough is firm but not dry.
6. Place dough in clean oiled bowl. Cover and place in warm breeze-free spot to rise.
7. When twice its original size, turn out onto floured board and form into loaves or rolls.
8. Let rise again. Then bake at 350 degrees for 20-30 minutes or until golden. Do not over bake. Let cool before slicing.

If you have half a mind to get married — do it.
A half a mind is all it takes.

August 19, 1910

Dear Emily,

You may tell Franklin that I do believe his six pound bass will indeed be the winner this time. Poor Andrew has had the worst stroke of bad luck. Last week he was replacing a shoe on Huey when a terrible accident occurred. Huey is such a passive animal that I was amazed a gartersnake could unnerve him so much. Huey jumped sideways knocking Andrew to the ground and then kicked blindly. Thank God Andrew had the presence of mind to shield his head with his arm, though the arm was badly broken by the impact. Doctor Torgeson set Andrew's arm and sewed 18 stitches into the gash near his shoulder. He wrapped the arm close to Andrew's body, and gave strict instructions that Andrew must be completely inactive for a minimum of six weeks. Andrew is furious and frustrated about the situation - - I am simply glad he is alive. This incident only serves to remind us all that no matter how careful we are around these massive animals, they are unpredictable, and that, in turn, causes them to be dangerous. Andrew's arm will mend and eventually be fine, but I am not so sure about our hay crop which is due to be harvested in less than a week.

As you are aware high farming costs and lower return prices, over the past two years have been a brutal blow to farms and ranches across the country. We simply cannot afford to loose this crop, Em. I know it must be on Andrew's mind, as well. He has not mentioned a word about it, but I can see the worry on his face. Last night I awoke to find him gone from our bed. He was out on the front porch in the moonlight looking out over his crop. I wished I could help him, but I knew I could not. I do, however, have great faith that all will work out for the best somehow. God never closes doors that he cannot open.

Keep us in your prayers, Em.

Love, Hannah

Home Sweet Home Rye Bread

Full of flavor and rich texture.

Makes 2 large loaves

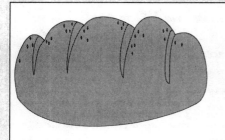

Dissolve sugar and yeast in water and set aside.

2 cups butter shortening
2 cups hot water
1/2 cup brown sugar
1/3 cup molasses
2 tsp. salt
2 cups rye flour
3-4 cups white flour

Ingredients:
2 Tbl. dry yeast
1/4 cup lukewarm water
1/2 tsp. sugar

Utensils:
2 large loaf pans
large mixing bowl
mixer

Putting it all together:

1. Combine shortening, water, molasses, sugar and salt in mixing bowl. Mix at low speed to dissolve.
2. Add rye flour and yeast mixture. Mix lightly.
3. Remove from mixer and turn dough out onto floured board. Mixture may be loose.
4. Knead in remaining flour or until dough is firm but not dry.
5. Place dough in clean oiled bowl. Cover and place in warm breeze-free spot to rise.
6. When twice its original size, turn out onto floured board and form into loaves or rolls.
7. Let rise again. Then bake at 350 degrees for 20-30 minutes or until golden. Do not over bake.
8. Serve warm from the oven or cool to slice.

A minor operation is one performed on someone else.

September 12, 1910
Dear Emily,

Even now, days later, the remembrance of the all those wagons and people coming down the road at dawn still thrills my heart, and causes my eyes to tear. I heard them while I was milking, Em — the clatter of wagon's wheels and the rhythmic vibrations of horses hooves. And then I heard the voices — men, and women, and even children, all loud and cheerful. I counted thirty-one wagons all in a line, progressing down our road. I was shouting for Andrew and Meg and by the time I reached the house everyone was pushing their way outside to see what was the matter. We stood on the porch, together with the girls, and watched them come. Fifty-seven people, some we did not even know, loaded with equipment and food, and all with willing hands.

Harvest day could have quietly come and gone with our crop still standing in the field, if it had not been for our wonderful friends and neighbors. It amazes me that with the tremendous amount work left to do on their own farms and ranches before winter, they came to help us. It took three days to do all the work that Andrew and I had been forced to forgo.

Emily, their tents set up all along the creek were an exciting sight each morning, and the sounds of people singing by the fire in the evening was comforting. From a distance, their lanterns lit the scene like as many twinkling stars.

On the last night, with the harvest complete, we all celebrated with a bit of impromptu amusement, storytelling, and dancing. And then the next day, with many hugs, best wishes, and prayers, we watched them go the way they came.

Tonight Andrew, Meg and I sat together on the porch after the girls were asleep. We looked out over our harvested fields, rows of stacked firewood, and equipment stored neatly for winter. We relived the events of the past few days and thanked God for our families and friends.

Lovingly, Hannah

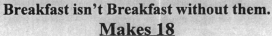

Easy English Muffins

Breakfast isn't Breakfast without them.
Makes 18

1 1/2 tsp. salt
1 tsp. dry yeast
1/2 cup powdered milk (dry)
2 cups warm water
3 Tbl. butter
cornmeal for dusting

Utensils:
large bowl
skillet
sauce pan

Ingredients:
5 -6 cups flour
3 Tbl. sugar

Putting it all together:

1. Combine 2 cups flour, sugar, salt and yeast in large bowl. Stir to blend.
2. In sauce pan, heat milk, water and butter. Cool to lukewarm.
3. Gradually stir in enough flour to make a soft dough. Knead dough on well floured surface adding flour until dough is smooth and firm, but not dry.
4. Form into ball and brush with oil. Place dough in bowl, cover and put in warm place to rise until double in size.
5. Roll out dough 1/2 inch thick and cut into 3 inch diameter rounds. (A round cookie cutter works good or just use a glass if you want).
6. Roll tops in cornmeal and place on cookie sheet cornmeal side up.
7. Cover and let rise again.
8. Fry muffins, cornmeal side down, for 5-6 minutes at medium heat until golden brown. Turn muffins over and fry other side.
9. Cool and store in air tight container. (These freeze well and this dough makes great pizza crust too!)

You know it's time to diet when you nod one chin and the others second the motion.

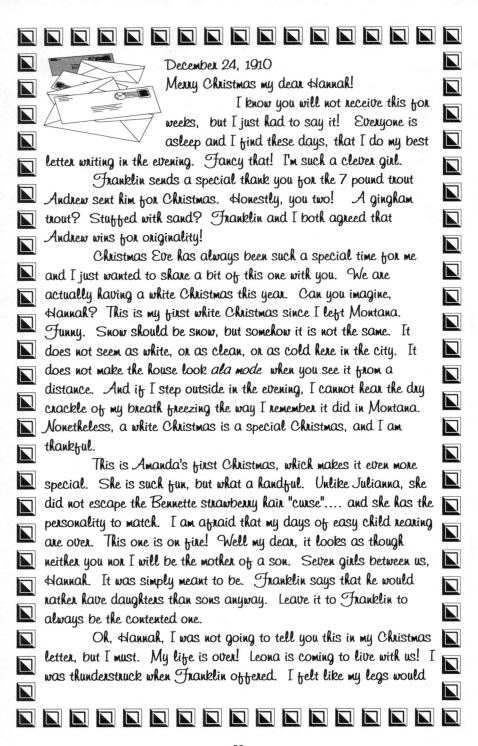

December 24, 1910

Merry Christmas my dear Hannah!

I know you will not receive this for weeks, but I just had to say it! Everyone is asleep and I find these days, that I do my best letter writing in the evening. Fancy that! I'm such a clever girl.

Franklin sends a special thank you for the 7 pound trout Andrew sent him for Christmas. Honestly, you two! A gingham trout? Stuffed with sand? Franklin and I both agreed that Andrew wins for originality!

Christmas Eve has always been such a special time for me and I just wanted to share a bit of this one with you. We are actually having a white Christmas this year. Can you imagine, Hannah? This is my first white Christmas since I left Montana. Funny. Snow should be snow, but somehow it is not the same. It does not seem as white, or as clean, or as cold here in the city. It does not make the house look *ala mode* when you see it from a distance. And if I step outside in the evening, I cannot hear the dry crackle of my breath freezing the way I remember it did in Montana. Nonetheless, a white Christmas is a special Christmas, and I am thankful.

This is Amanda's first Christmas, which makes it even more special. She is such fun, but what a handful. Unlike Julianna, she did not escape the Bennette strawberry hair "curse".... and she has the personality to match. I am afraid that my days of easy child rearing are over. This one is on fire! Well my dear, it looks as though neither you nor I will be the mother of a son. Seven girls between us, Hannah. It was simply meant to be. Franklin says that he would rather have daughters than sons anyway. Leave it to Franklin to always be the contented one.

Oh, Hannah, I was not going to tell you this in my Christmas letter, but I must. My life is over! Leona is coming to live with us! I was thunderstruck when Franklin offered. I felt like my legs would

South of the Border Cornbread

A little spicy, but too delicious to pass up!
<u>Serves 18</u>

Ingredients:
1 1/2 cups yellow cornmeal
1 cup flour
3 tsp. baking powder
1 tsp. baking soda
1 tsp. salt
12 oz. canned corn
1 lg. grated onion
6 chopped jalapeno chilis
(don't forget to seed them!
Yikes!)
2 cups milk
1/2 cup honey
1/2 cup vegetable oil

4 eggs

Utensils:
large mixing bowl
mixer
9 X 13 baking pan

Putting it all together:

1. Blend eggs, honey, salt, oil, onion, chiles, and milk.
2. Add cornmeal, flour, baking soda and baking powder. Stir lightly and fold in corn.
3. Pour batter into well greased baking dish.
4. Bake at 350 degrees for 30 minutes or until cornbread tests done in center.
5. Cool 5 minutes. Cut and serve.

My mother suffers in
silence louder than anyone I know.

51

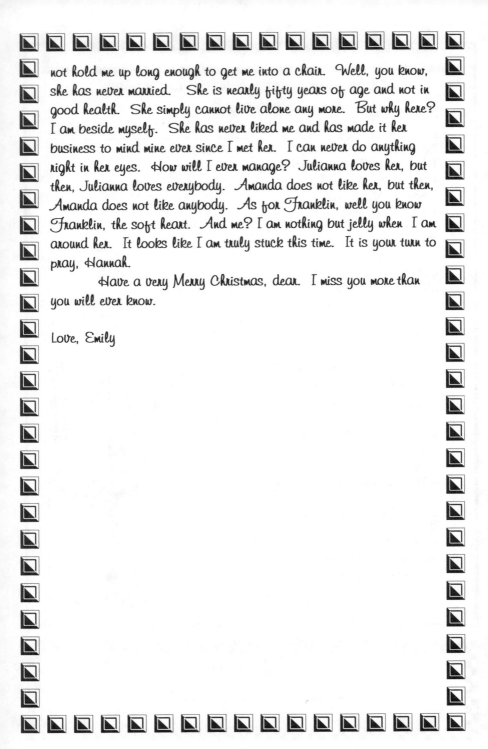

not hold me up long enough to get me into a chair. Well, you know, she has never married. She is nearly fifty years of age and not in good health. She simply cannot live alone any more. But why here? I am beside myself. She has never liked me and has made it her business to mind mine ever since I met her. I can never do anything right in her eyes. How will I ever manage? Julianna loves her, but then, Julianna loves everybody. Amanda does not like her, but then, Amanda does not like anybody. As for Franklin, well you know Franklin, the soft heart. And me? I am nothing but jelly when I am around her. It looks like I am truly stuck this time. It is your turn to pray, Hannah.

Have a very Merry Christmas, dear. I miss you more than you will ever know.

Love, Emily

Down Home Buttermilk Biscuits

Light, fluffy, moist — Yum!
<u>Makes 18</u>

Ingredients:
3 cups flour
1 Tbl. sugar
2 Tbl. baking soda
1 tsp. salt
3/4 cup butter flavored
shortening

2 cups buttermilk

Utensils:
cookie sheet
mixing bowl

Putting it all together:

1. Mix together flour, baking soda, sugar, and salt.
2. Cut in shortening to make a crumbly meal-like texture.
3. Add buttermilk and toss lightly to mix. (Do not stir. A fluffy tender biscuit is one that is handled at a minimum.)
4. Turn out onto a floured board and gently roll dough to 1 inch thick.
5. Cut with round biscuit cutter.
6. Place on well greased cookie sheet and bake at 375 degrees for 10-15 minutes or until lightly golden. Do not over bake.
7. Serve right from the oven with butter and honey.

A vacation is what you take when you can no longer take what you've been taking.

April 10, 1917

Dear Hannah,

I am certain that by now you have heard the dreadful news. America has gone to war, and on Good Friday, no less! All our hopes of staying out of this hideous European mess have been dashed. Already, all around us here in the south, young men are enlisting to fight. How thankful I am that I have no sons, though we have several friends and acquaintances whose sons are anxious to go. Franklin says that ships are being sent to Charleston to carry our khaki clad boys across the Atlantic. How I hate to see this happening. How can it be? I suppose we all should have known war was just around the corner with Britain's Lusitania sunk off its own coast by the Germans. As you recall, 1,100 lives were lost. Over 100 Americans were aboard that ship and died with the rest. Public sympathy has not lent itself to forgive ever since, and now we are at war.

It is strange the sense of jubilation I feel all around us here. As if the thought of war has breathed excitement into the air. I, however, am feeling a sense of dread, and am praying that peace will return as quickly as it departed.

Love,

Emily

Glorious Morning Muffins

A delicious brunch or breakfast treat!

Makes 24

Ingredients:
1 - 2 cups flour
3/4 cup sugar
1/4 cup brown sugar
2 tsp. baking soda
2 1/4 tsp. ground cinnamon
1/2 tsp. salt
2/3 cup raisins
2 cups grated carrots
1 lg. tart apple shredded
1/2 cup chopped almonds
1/3 cup flake coconut
2 eggs beaten
1/2 cup vegetable oil
1/2 cup applesauce

2 tsp. vanilla
1/4 tsp lemon extract
1 cup milk
hot water

Utensils:
muffin tin
mixing bowl

Putting it all together:

1. Soak raisins in enough hot water to cover for 30 minutes. Set aside.
2. Mix together 1 cup flour, sugars, baking soda, cinnamon and salt.
3. Stir in raisins and remaining ingredients.
4. Add flour as needed to achieve batter consistency. (Batter should be a little thicker than cake batter.)
5. Spoon into well greased muffin tins. Bake at 350 degrees for 20-30 minutes or until golden. Do not over bake.
6. Cool and store in air tight container or freeze to use later.

Who says I say all those things they say I say?

Thanksgiving Day 1917
Dear Emily,

After all the hubbub of the day I needed some time to myself and I have retreated to the comfort of my bedroom to linger over a letter to you. It hardly seems like we should be celebrating the holidays with the war raging on, and our boys so far away from home.

Dorothy Howe's youngest son, Theo, has been killed. I am sure you must remember him, and Pansy Miller's son, Emery, is missing in action. I cannot fathom the pain these mothers must feel, nor can I imagine the loss of a child to violent death. We must all pray for a speedy end to this war.

All in all, I found it difficult to be truly thankful today, though Meg reminded me of all we certainly do have to be thankful for. Still, I have not felt this blue since Augie died in the spring. I feel so lonely without him. I took him for granted like a comfortable pair of shoes, but I miss him terribly. Don't I sound awful. Let me try to think of something else.

We have new neighbors, Em. Rudyard and Margaret McCleary have bought Marshall's old place. They are a delightful young couple -- he calls her Peg and she calls him Rud. They have an infant son, Ethan, and another baby on the way. The McClearys have moved here all the way from Nebraska where, tragically, their house, barn, and crop burned last summer in a prairie brush fire. Rudyard said they were lucky to escape with their lives, and did so by hiding in the root cellar, under the house, until the fire had passed. When they came out, they found everything gone -- burned to the ground. They left Nebraska with only the clothes on their backs and the money they had in the bank. Margaret told me they could not face starting over among the ashes of their old life. The McCleary's decision to come north to Montana was based on nothing more than the unseen promise of abundance and the hope of a bountiful new life. Such brave people, these Nebraskans. They have managed to buy the Marshall's land outright, and have built a one room shelter for the winter. Andrew and I are guessing that their money is about

Bran Muffins by the Pailful

**These are terrific! Make the batter and keep it
in the refrigerator for up to two weeks.
Bake a few fresh muffins every morning!**
<u>Makes 48</u>

Ingredients:
4 cups all bran buds
2 cups rolled oats
1 tsp. salt
2 cups boiling water
4 cups buttermilk
4 beaten eggs
1 cup oil
2-3 cups mixed chopped dried
fruit and nuts (Raisins, dates,
walnuts, pecans etc.-whatever.

Choose what you like best!)
1 cup applesauce
1 cup sugar
5 cups sifted flour
5 tsp. baking soda

Utensils:
large covered plastic
container,
large mixing bowl,
muffin tins

Putting it all together:

1. Mix together first four ingredients.
Stir well and cool.
2. Add buttermilk, eggs, oil, sugar,
dried fruit and nuts.
3. Stir together.
4. Add remaining ingredients.
5. Stir again, cover and store in
refrigerator until ready to use.
To Bake:
Spoon into well greased muffin tins
and bake at 350 degrees for 15-20
minutes or until done.

*God made woman beautiful so man
would love her — and then He made woman
foolish so she would love man.*

gone, but we will share what we have and they will make it through just fine.

The McClearys were here for Thanksgiving dinner today, and what a feast it was. Margaret certainly understands what a kitchen is used for, and she and I had a marvelous time building a meal to be remembered. Meg enjoyed us thundering around in her kitchen. She doesn't cook much any more and I think she really enjoys seeing a traditional holiday dinner being produced.

Yes, I surely do have much for which to be thankful. As Meg would say, "look at what you have not what you don't."

Lovingly, Hannah

Butterscotch-Orange Muffins

Melt in your mouth Muffins for your sweet tooth.
<u>Makes a dozen</u>

Ingredients:
Topping:
6 oz. butterscotch chips
1 Tbl. butter
1/2 cup flour

Muffins:
1 1/2 cups flour
1/2 cup sugar
2 Tbl. baking powder
1/2 tsp. salt
1/2 tsp. cinnamon
1/4 tsp. nutmeg
6 oz. butterscotch chips
1/4 cup milk
1/4 cup orange juice
1/4 cup vegetable oil
1 egg
1 tsp. orange zest (optional)

Utensils:
Muffin tins
mixer and mixing bowl

Putting it all together:

Topping:
Melt butter and chips in microwave or over low heat. Cut in flour to make crumbly mixture.

Muffins:
1. Combine dry ingredients in mixing bowl.
2. Add milk, oil, egg, orange juice and orange zest. Mix well.
3. Fold in butterscotch chips.
4. Spoon into well greased muffin tins. (Fill about 3/4 full.)
5. Sprinkle topping on each muffin.
6. Bake at 350 degrees for 15 - 20 minutes. Do not over bake.

When you quit having birthdays, you're dead.

July 7, 1918

Dear Emily,

Happy birthday in just a few short days, my dear friend. I suppose it is not polite to suggest age to a Southern lady. So sorry.

We have had such a busy spring and though the girls are very helpful, this ranch has grown so big in the past few years that we can hardly keep up with it all. Babe and Mary Ella had birthdays, as well, and they decided to celebrate their sixteenth and fifteenth birthdays together this year on Independence Day (though one was born in March and the other in April). Silly really, but they invited all their friends for a big outdoor party. The girls made most of the food and all of the decorations themselves, and I was proud of them for getting through the party, and its preparations, without an argument. Beth will be thirteen in October and Ruth and Clare just turned eleven in May. It is quite a brood we have, and they are still a handful, but in different ways than when they were little. It used to be that "no" simply meant "no", without question. Andrew maintains his position as the "final word" in our household, but only by a small margin, and I have concluded that child rearing was much easier when I did not have to justify or rationalize my requests and decisions. The girls have all turned into such lovely young women though Em, and I am proud to claim them. Their personalities are still as different as the colors of the rainbow --as is only natural I suppose, but I find Beth to be by far the most complex.

Beth is our "little rancher" and always the protector of every animal. A year ago last spring one of Andrew's longhorns birthed a fine bull and then promptly died. Andrew felt the bull, though very small, was worth saving, and guess who volunteered to raise it? Beth named him Bambino.

Beth proved to be a dedicated nursemaid and raised the young bull on milk, and later added pancakes to his diet. Since I prepare pancakes nearly every day for breakfast, it seemed to

60

Rocky Mountain Gingerbread

This has been in the family for years. A personal favorite.

Makes 1 large loaf

Ingredients:

1/4 cup butter flavored
shortening or butter
1/4 cup white sugar
1/2 cup molasses
1/2 tsp. baking soda
1 tsp. each: cinnamon, ginger,
cloves and salt
1/2 tsp. allspice
1 1/4 cups flour
1 tsp. baking powder
1 beaten egg
3/4 cup boiling water
1/4 tsp. baking soda

Utensils:

Mixing bowl and mixer
large loaf pan

Putting it all together:

1. Cream the sugar and butter or shortening.
2. Sift together all dry ingredients, except baking soda.
3. Beat 1/2 tsp. baking soda into molasses until fluffy. Add to sugar and butter mixture.
4. Add 1/4 tsp. baking soda to the boiling water. Add this alternately with the dry ingredients to the molasses mixture.
5. Fold in beaten egg.
6. Pour into greased loaf pan (the batter will be thin) and bake for 30 minutes at 400 degrees.
7. Remove from oven and let cool for 15 minutes. Then invert pan and remove bread. Finish cooling on rack. Store in covered container.
8. Serve smothered in lemon curd. To die for!

The only reason that some brides promise to love, honor and obey is that they don't want to start an argument in front of all those people.

Beth that this should be the sensible dietary supplement for her bull. It was indeed.

Within a year Bambino was enormous, which is not common for the longhorn breed, but this bull was big and spoiled -- coming right onto the porch and up to the kitchen door for his pancakes!

Andrew tried several times to convince Beth that the bull should be sold with the other yearling stock, but she was attached to Bambino by this time and persuaded her father to keep him at least temporarily. Andrew agreed, but insisted that bull become steer in the interim.

Bambino got bigger and beefier as the months went by and Andrew became more and more annoyed by a steer becoming so familiar with his back porch. But Beth and Bambino were big buddies. He followed her everywhere and she continued to spoil him. Rudyard said he was positive the big bovine thought Beth was his mother.

The end came when Andrew stepped out onto the back porch one sunny June morning, coffee cup in hand, to greet the day. He was, instead, greeted by a cow pie -- or rather a steer pie in this case. This would not have been so unfortunate had he discovered it before he stepped in it -- and had he been wearing shoes. Andrew, a man slow to anger, was angry.

The valley ranchers had been organizing a big cattle drive to the Yellowstone for nearly a year and the round-up was completed. They would be leaving in five days, and Bambino would be going with them. Needless to say, going without Beth's consent. Tempers flared, and father and daughter exploded into an argument that could be heard all the way from the barn to the house. Beth lost the battle, though she stubbornly walked with Bambino, and the great herd, the five miles to the outer border of our ranch. She cried and cried for days and would not talk to her father for many more.

When the men returned from the cattle drive in August they told Andrew that they had experienced trouble with that miserable steer from the first day. He would turn back given any opportunity, and they never truly convinced him to follow the herd.

Cinnamon Spiced Apple Bread

A delicious treat with a spicy aroma.

Ingredients:
2 cups flour
1/2 cup white sugar
3 tsp. baking powder
1/2 tsp. cinnamon
1/2 tsp. salt
1/2 cup butter
1 small apple peeled and diced
1 cup applesauce

1 cup walnuts finely chopped
1 egg
2/3 cup milk
Topping:
1 tsp. cinnamon
2 Tbl. brown sugar
Utensils:
large mixing bowl
2 medium loaf pans
cup of apple spice tea for the
very hard working cook

Putting it all together:
1. Sift flour, sugar, baking powder, 1/2 tsp cinnamon and salt into large bowl.
2. Cut in butter with pastry cutter. Then measure out 1/4 cup and reserve for topping.
3. Add apple and nuts to flour mixture.
4. Stir in egg and milk (batter will be lumpy).
5. Spoon into greased loaf pans.
6. Add 1 tsp. cinnamon and 2 Tbl. brown sugar to reserved topping mixture. Sprinkle over batter evenly.
7. Bake at 350 degrees for 15 to 20 minutes or until loaves test done.
8. Remove from oven and let cool for 15 minutes. Then invert pan and remove bread. Finish cooling on rack. Store in covered container.
8. Slather with applesauce and a touch of nutmeg.

Why is it that the bride always looks stunning and the groom just looks stunned?

The men said they had to drive Bambino all the way to Wyoming, and had a terrible time keeping track of him. The herd was delivered safely, sold and slaughtered. This should have been the end of the story, but it was not.

Yesterday morning a tired, weak, and badly scarred Bambino stumbled up onto the back porch and bellowed for Beth. Beth recognized his voice immediately and raced out onto the porch. She fed him the pancakes right off her plate, put her arms around his big neck, and cried happy tears. It was quite a sight. That monster of an animal had traveled hundreds of miles through rivers, and fences, and winter, and over at least one mountain pass to get home to Beth. He stood there on the porch and drank in her affection and then followed quietly to the barn as if nothing had ever happened.

Andrew agreed that Beth had won, and that Bambino has a home for life. Life is never dull.

Goodbye for now and congratulations to Amanda on her music award.

Love, Hannah

Breakfast

November 27, 1918
Dear Hannah,

I am writing you with the happiest of birthday wishes since I can gleefully say that after all these horrific months the war is over. Yes indeed, President Wilson, it shall be a war to end all wars. Franklin and I took the girls and they were at the dock to watch many of our doughboys come home to friendly soil. It was an exciting time to see familiar faces coming back, though it was also a heart wrenching time watching mothers and wives meeting men and boys who came ashore on stretchers, or crutches, or worse. We watched hopeful people desperately searching the faces in the crowd for ones they recognized; looking for sons and husbands that were not there. So many were killed and buried in unmarked graves, and many more are unaccounted for. My friends, Martha Scott and Georgia Edmonds, lost their sons. Felicity Holme's boy came home without a leg, and Drucilla Pendleton's son was blinded. Though I tried, I was not, and am not, able to comfort them. Their loss is too great.

My dear Aunt Beatrice is very ill, Hannah, and I fear I will lose her. She is very old now, and is confined to a wheel chair. Her memory has become slippery and she has lost all appetite, even for her most favorite foods. I know it is the natural course of events to live, and grow old, and to die, but I dread Aunt Beatrice's passing. She has so loved me; as I have her. Uncle Edward is coming to be with her, but he will be 72 in May and I can't imagine he will be able to travel much longer; at least in the manner he is used to doing. I look at him and see a man still reasonably fit, where Aunt Beatrice, who is close to the same age, seems so frail.

Franklin brought home the sweetest kitten the other day. I am sure he did so to take my mind off Aunt Beatrice. The kitten is fluffy white with the prettiest blue eyes, and I named her Minute. She follows me everywhere during the day, but prefers to sleep with Amanda at night, which I consider desertion.

Franklin has taken a liking to cats ever since his mother

High Country Buttermilk Flapjacks

"Yum" spoken here.

Makes 6 - 8 inch pancakes

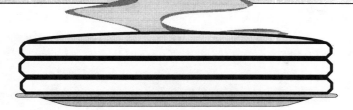

Ingredients:
3 cups flour
1/4 cup rolled oats
3 Tbl. baking powder
1/2 cup sugar
1/4 cup oil
1 tsp. vanilla

1/4 tsp. almond extract
2 - 3 cups buttermilk

Utensils:
large skillet or griddle
mixing bowl
ladle

Putting it all together:

1. Soak oats in buttermilk for 15 minutes.
2. In a large bowl mix flour, sugar and baking powder
3. Add oil, buttermilk mixture and extracts.
4. Stir to blend. Mixture should be the consistency of cake batter.
5. Ladle onto HOT griddle or skillet. (The amount will depend on the size pancake you prefer.)
6. When pancake bubbles (about 1 minute), flip over and brown on opposite side for 15 seconds.
7. Drench in butter, your favorite topping or syrup. Eat your fill and have a nap.

When a youngster hears a bad word
it ususally goes in one ear and out his mouth.

suggested he get one for his shop; to control the mice. Mother Sawyer gave him her fat old yellow cat, Maurice, to be Franklin's shop companion and mouse chaser. She said he was a good mouser, though I think he sleeps better than he hunts. Maurice and Franklin quite fancy each other, however, and they make an inseparable pair during business hours. Maurice lounges on the counter or drapes himself over Franklin's shoulder most of the day. George Rawlins, who owns the shoe store next to Franklin's shop, affectionately calls them, "Feline and Frankline". George likes to make disparaging remarks about Maurice's lack of hunting prowess, and though his remarks are playful, Franklin often warns George that Maurice understands every word. Yesterday Franklin's warnings rang true. George had come over mid-afternoon to have a cup of coffee with Franklin. Maurice was asleep on the counter as usual, and George, not wanting to miss an opportunity, mentioned loudly that he could see Maurice was busily at work keeping the rodent population in check. Maurice opened a sleepy eye, lazily got to his feet, stretched and yawned. Then he strolled down the counter and hopped onto George's lap. Franklin was about to ask George to make note of what a forgiving sort his cat was, when Maurice retched and then regurgitated a half digested mouse onto the front of George Rawlin's shirt. Revolting, to say the least.

Satisfied with himself, Maurice hopped off his victim's lap and strolled back down the counter where he resumed his nap. Though I find this story vulgar Franklin loves to repeat it, especially if George is within ear shot. How their friendship survives all this banter is beyond me.

Speaking of George Rawlins, his son Mitchell was a flyer in the war; one of the few that escaped harm. Franklin is planning to invite Mitchell, along with George, and Cornelia, for supper when he gets home. I am anticipating an exciting evening where I am sure Mitchell's tales of flying will have us hanging on every word.

Have a wonderful birthday my dear "old" friend.

Love, Em

The Original Belgium Waffle

Like nothing you have ever tasted.
Makes 12 waffles

Ingredients:
2 Tbl. dry yeast
1 3/4 cups warm water
2 cups evaporated milk
8 eggs separated
1 tsp. vanilla extract
1 tsp. almond extract
5 cups flour
1 tsp. salt
2 Tbl. ugar
1 cup melted butter

Utensils:
waffle iron
mixing bowl
cooking spray
ladle

Putting it all together:

1. Beat egg yolks. Add extracts and milk.
2. Combine flour, sugar, yeast and salt and add to egg mixture.
3. Stir in warm water and melted butter.
4. Beat whites until fluffy and fold into batter.
5. Spray heated waffle iron and ladle in correct amount of batter.
6. Do not over cook.

If a kid is spoiled it's probably because you can't spank grandmothers.

April 22, 1920

Dear Emily,

The funniest thing happened last week. I was sitting looking out the window one morning watching what I thought was surely the last snow fall of the winter. The children were all in school. Andrew had gone over to Billy Johnston's to look at a brood mare and I had just poured myself a cup of tea. I was lost in some sort of silly daydream when I saw something moving out of the corner of my eye. I got up and went to the kitchen door. I opened it and stepped outside — wearing nothing but my house dress mind you. I did not see anything unusual, so I leaned around the corner of the house to get a better look. Emily, have you ever seen a moose close up? I mean really close up? They are big — very big. Take my word for it, and this particular moose was not more than 18 inches from my face. I was so scared that I could not utter a scream, which of course, meant that I could not move either. So, like a dummy, I just stood there shivering in the cold, or trembling with fear. I am not sure which.

Her eyes were like two black lumps of coal and they got wider as she breathed harder. She took a step forward. I took one backward. The scene repeated itself. And then she came right up on the porch after me. Well, let me tell you, I was beyond "mad scramble" long before I got to the kitchen door and hysterical by the time I was behind it. The moose was just plain mad. Imagine the nerve of that beast to smash the glass in my brand new kitchen door! Well, then I got mad. I snatched Andrew's rifle from behind the wood box, closed my eyes and fired. The look on Andrew's face! A semi-demolished kitchen door and a completely dead moose. Not exactly two birds with one stone. The children are having great fun with this story and Frank Miller called me Annie Oakley when I was in the feed store last week. Cheeky bugger.

Anyway, this whole thing is truly funny now. Reminded me of Bud and Phyllis Baker and their "bear on the porch" story. You remember, Em. Same sort of thing, except Bud ended up on

Oven-baked French Toast

Quick and easy — a real winner!

Serves 6

Ingredients:
1 loaf of sliced bread
(any kind of bread is good,
whatever your favorite, and
day old is best!)

6 eggs beaten
2 cups milk
1 tsp. vanilla
1 tsp. rum extract
1/2 cup sugar
1/4 cup butter
1 tsp. cinnamon
1/2 tsp. nutmeg

Utensils:
Chilled glass baking dish
(11 X 13)
large bowl

Putting it all together:

1. Melt butter and coat bottom of chilled baking dish. Return to refrigerator.
2. Beat eggs, milk, extracts and sugar together.
3. Pour 1/2 of milk mixture into baking dish.
4. Lay bread in bottom of baking dish.
5. Pour remaining milk mixture over bread. Sprinkle with cinnamon and nutmeg.
6. Cover and refrigerate over night.
7. In the morning, heat oven to 375 degrees and bake french toast for 30 minutes or until golden and edges are crispy.
8. I don't think I have to tell you what to do next. Enjoy!

The closest to perfection anyone woman comes is when she writes her resume'.

the porch with a .22 rifle -- like trying to kill an elephant with a sling-shot. Phyllis panicked and shut the door when the bear charged. Poor Bud was running backwards and trying to shoot the intruder at the same time. All the racket he made falling over the chair and then through the railing of the porch scared the bear off, I guess. He was lying on the ground, stuck in the broken railing, and he was so mad at Phyllis for laughing at him that he swore he was going to feed her to the next bear he saw.

Well, I would not have believed it if I hadn't heard it straight from Doc Torgeson's own lip's yesterday. I'm pregnant again. Or am I expecting? I can never remember which. Wouldn't you just know it. They say "never give your baby clothes and diapers away, because you will surely get pregnant." I did and I am. Andrew and the girls want a boy. I just want it to be healthy, but if it is a boy, I'll be thrilled. This one should be born around the first of September. Six children, Emily! People will think we have no self control what-so-ever! Andrew said he knew a month ago. He says my cheeks get pink. How embarrassing. Goodbye for now, Emily.

Love, Hannah

Land of Nod Sticky Buns

Before you put the cat out for the night, make these easy rolls and in the morning dazzle your guests.

<u>Serves 6</u>

Ingredients:

20 pieces frozen roll dough
1 cup brown
sugar
1/4 cup vanilla
instant pudding
mix (dry)
3/4 cup raisins
1/2 cup butter
2 tsp. cinnamon

Utensils:

bundt pan
cooking spray

Putting it all together:

1. Spray bundt pan with cooking spray.
2. Places frozen rolls (still hard frozen) in the bottom of the bundt pan.
3. Sprinkle with brown sugar, pudding, raisins and cinnamon.
4. Melt butter and pour over top.
5. Cover with a clean dish towel and place in cool oven.
6. Go to bed.
7. In the morning, remove the dish towel, and turn the oven on to 350 degrees. (No need to pre-heat the oven). Bake about 20 minutes or until rolls turn lightly golden.
8. Turn immediately out onto a plate and serve hot.

*Success is relative —
the more success the more relatives.*

July 19, 1920
Dearest Hannah,
   No self control indeed! I've been telling you that for years — and you said it was fun, but that you were finished! Maybe you should have read that book of Doctor Torgeson's instead of throwing it down the privy hole! Ho! Ho! Ho! Forgive me. I could not help myself.

Love, Emily

September 5, 1920
Dear Emily,
   Andrew and I have a son, though I never dreamed it possible. After all these girls who would have thought we could do it. What a handsome lad he is -- the very image of his father.
   Andrew David Hansen, Jr. is quite a handle for my perfect little man. He was a big baby -- nearly ten pounds, and I struggled to deliver him for over fifteen hours. I was so exhausted at the last, that Doctor Toregeson had to finally make me angry, to give me that final surge of energy I needed to push. When it was all over, I told him he had the bedside manner of Atilla the Hun. He laughed.
   Andrew was worried. He told me later that he feared he might lose me. There was the odd moment that I thought he would lose me too, though I did not say so.
   And then there he was, our little boy, my prize for all my hard work. Perfect in every way, strong and loud, and full of the life God gave him. Andrew and I are proud of ourselves. We did a very good job.

Love, Hannah

Rise n' Shine Fruit Salad

This mixed fruit bowl is the perfect compliment to any breakfast menu.

<u>Serves 8</u>

Ingredients:

1 cup fruit flavored (lemon, tangerine, blueberry etc.) or vanilla yogurt
4 cups chopped fruit (seedless grapes, melon balls, banana, strawberries, kiwi. Choose your favorites)
1/2 cup raisins
1/2 cup chopped dates
1 cup miniature marshmallows
1/4 cup pineapple juice
2 Tbl. shredded coconut
1 tsp. cinnamon
dash nutmeg

Utensils:

large salad bowl
chilled fruit plates

Putting it all together:

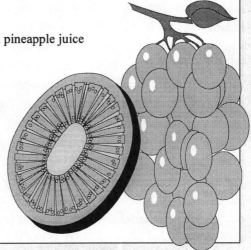

1.   Soak raisins and dates in pineapple juice for 15 minutes.
2. Whisk cinnamon and nutmeg into yogurt.
3. Toss raisin mixture and yogurt mixture with fruit coconut and marshmallows.
4. Serve immediately on chilled plates.

Love is like a mushroom — you never know if it's the real thing until it's too late.

February 3, 1921

Dear Hannah,

Finally a boy! I can just imagine Andrew. Will you ever be able to wipe the grin off his face? Andrew David Hansen, Jr. What an impressive name. Oh, please do not call him A.J., Hannah. I know how you love nicknames, but a handsome little lad should not have to answer to a name with no structure. A.J. sounds like a gangster or someones pet, for heaven's sake. Your beautiful Augusta called "Babe", of all things. And then you took a wonderful name like Elizabeth Ann Marie and shortened it to "Beth." And now A.J.? If you ever have another one, you probably will not bother to name it at all.

Franklin's business is growing by leaps and bounds. He is working much too hard and I worry about his health. He seems happier than I have ever seen him, though. Perhaps some people thrive on hard work and busy schedules. I am definitely not one of them. I know I should take the word "yes" out of my vocabulary, and I do say no, but nobody listens. Now don't start, Hannah. You have admonished me more than once on this very issue. Old habits are hard to break. This year, I am on the board of The Ladies Aid Society and three other charities. In addition, I am chairwoman of the Church Social Committee. I take Amanda with me as often as possible, and though she is a constant source of public embarrassment, I find her antics quite humorous. What a character she is! She reminds me of you, Hannah. As a matter of fact, her assertive nature and her annoying habit of "speaking her mind" are exactly like you. I thank God that you are not here to influence her.

In your last letter, you asked about Leona. She still infuriates me daily, and for a while I thought she would drive me mad. I felt like a prisoner in my own home, but then something happened that has changed my view of Leona considerably. I was in the kitchen drying dishes and muttering under my breath about something nasty Leona had said to me. Julianna was sitting quietly on the window seat listening to my fuming. I suppose I stopped long enough to take a breath and Julianna gently

Hannah's Breakfast Souffle'

Lighter than air with delicate herb flavors.
Serves 4

Ingredients:
10 eggs
1 cup milk
1/4 cup crumbled bacon
cooked crisp
1/4 cup fresh Parmesan
cheese shredded
1/4 cup sharp cheddar cheese
shredded
1/4 cup mozzarella cheese
shredded
1/4 cup chopped shitake
mushrooms
1/4 cup chopped sun-dried
tomatoes

2 green onions chopped
1 tsp. summer savory
1/4 tsp. dried lavender
1 tsp. garlic powder
dash of pepper
Utensils:
1 qt. crockery or
glass souffle' dish
mixing bowl
wire whisk

Putting it all together:

1. Spray Souffle dish with cooking spray.
2. Whisk together eggs, pepper, dried lavender, summer savory and milk and pour into souffle' dish.
3. Sprinkle with remaining ingredients in the following order: bacon, onions, mushrooms, tomatoes, and cheeses.
4. Bake at 325 degrees for 15 minutes and 425 degrees for 5 more minutes or until center tests done.
5. Serve immediately. (Great when it's hot and not when it's not.)

Tired of wrinkles — iron your face.

seized the opportunity to say something she must have been trying to say to me for months. She said, "Mama, Auntie Lee doesn't have any friends. She is so unhappy and she doesn't feel good most of the time. Couldn't you be her friend?" Out of the mouths of babes. She was right, of course. I have always tried to avoid Leona rather than include her. How awful this must have made her feel. I put down the dish towel and took a brisk walk up the stairs to Leona's room. Hannah, I did not bother to knock. I just walked in. Leona was sitting by the window in that blue velvet chair that she always favors. She turned and glared at me with that cold stare that normally wilts me. I took a deep breath and gathered my courage. "Leona," I said. "Would you like to go with me to the church bazaar on Friday? I think it would be great fun, and afterwards perhaps we could go to The Cranston for lunch." I was not prepared for the tears either of us shed that morning. It was as though years of aggravation and heartache melted away. Make no mistake. We still have our tense moments, Leona and I. But life is easier. The real change being that we tend to argue to finish the problem, rather than fuming privately. Thank God for the love and faith of children.

I will close for now. Franklin is coming up the walk. How do I know? I can hear him whistling!

All the best to all of yours, especially that precious Andrew David Hansen, Jr.

Love, Emily

Creamy Eggs Denmark

Smooth and creamy. A hearty breakfast favorite.
<u>Serves 6</u>

<u>*Ingredients:*</u>
2 Tbl. butter
2 Tbl. flour
1 tsp. salt
1 tsp. garlic powder
1 tsp. onion powder
1/2 tsp. cayenne pepper
8 hard boiled eggs peeled and
coarse chopped
1 cup jack cheese

1/2 cup bacon cooked crispy
and crumbled
1 cup sour cream
2 cups milk
6 English muffins halved,
buttered, and toasted

<u>*Utensils:*</u>
2 qt. sauce pan
wire whisk

<u>*Putting it all together:*</u>

1. In sauce pan over low heat, melt butter and stir in flour to make paste.
2. Slowly add milk, stirring constantly with wire whisk. Heat until mixture thickens, but do not boil.
3. Add all remaining ingredients except muffins, eggs, and bacon and stir to blend spices and melt cheese.
4. Gently stir in eggs.
5. Spoon over toasted muffins and sprinkle with bacon.
6. Serve hot.

The trouble with kids is that when they're not being a lump in the throat they're being a pain in the neck!

April 6, 1922

Dear Emily,

My Augusta Rose was married today. Clayton is a admirable young man. As you recall he is a lawyer with family ties to old money in San Francisco. He is exactly the man she had been waiting for. Someone to get her away from the country and into the city. Make no mistake, it was obvious today that my daughter loved the man with whom she exchanged vows, though I can not help but wonder if her future with Clayton was more attractive than Clayton himself. Now they are off to San Francisco to start their life together. His family is there waiting for them, and I know Augusta will be happy, and accepted, and will thrive in her new environment -- the environment that she always felt she was born to.

I will miss her. If the truth were told she and I raised each other. I was so young and inexperienced when she was born and all her life she was the first to teach me new things. Emily, as I watched her walk down the aisle on her father's arm this morning, I could not help but rest my hand on the new life secretly growing inside me. (Secretly until now, that is.) It was an awkward moment for me to realize that today as one child married, another was yet to be born. I am thirty-seven years of age and am not excited about raising a seventh child, but as I write this, and as God is my witness I know that there is something very special about this baby.

With love, Hannah

Huckleberry Coffee Cake

Moist and not too sweet. This coffee cake is a winner!
<u>Serves 10</u>

Ingredients:
4 eggs separated
1 3/4 cups sugar
3 tsp. vanilla
1/4 cup oil
1/2 cup sour cream
the juice of 2 fresh lemons
2 Tbl. of grated lemon rind
2 1/2 cups flour
2 tsp. baking powder
2 cups frozen huckleberries (or
blueberries) floured

Utensils:
bundt cake pan or 10 inch
spring form pan
cooking spray
mixing bowl

Putting it all together:

1. Beat egg whites until frothy.
2. Continue beating whites while adding sugar (gradually), egg yolks, oil, vanilla, sour cream, lemon juice and rind.
3. Fold in dry ingredients and 3/4 cup floured berries.
4. Scatter remaining berries in bottom of bundt pan.
5. Pour in batter and bake at 350 degrees for 1 hour or until cake tests done.
6. When cool, turn out onto cake plate and take a bow! (and a bite!)

*When choosing between the best of two evils,
choose the one you have never done before.*

November 1, 1922
Dear Em,

　　　　　I put the lamp in the window,
and I saw Andrew go, but he did not find
Doctor Torgeson in town. The doctor was
delivering Rowena Hardwig's baby girl—
her first, his eighty-second.

　　　And so while Andrew was gone, a very tiny Patrick
Michael Hansen was born. He was so fragile looking with
miniature fingers and toes, and a heavy sound in his chest. I
knew he was early, at least a month, but I suppose it never
crossed my mind that I might have a sick baby or worse one that
would not survive. All my babies have been so healthy and
strong. I just was not ready for Patrick.

　　　The girls bathed him and wrapped him warmly, but I
could not get him to nurse - - he was simply too weak. Beth even
warmed some goat's milk and tried to feed him a bit with an eye-
dropper, but he did not take much.

　　　Within an hour Andrew was home, shocked to see the
birth complete and distressed over his sick baby son. He took
Patrick from me and carried him to the kitchen where he laid the
baby in my bread basket, and set the basket on the open stove door
in an attempt to keep him warm. I was afraid we were losing
him, and felt helpless to save my little boy.

　　　Doctor Torgeson arrived near midnight and I could tell
that he was terribly concerned about the baby's condition.
Frustration and helplessness were evident on his face, and it was
obvious that there was no magical healing he could perform on our
son.

　　　At 3:00 AM, Patrick's breathing was very heavy and I
could hear a slight gurgle in his chest. His fingers and toes were
cold, and his lips the slightest shade of blue.

　　　We were all anxious - - fearing the worst and praying
that God would somehow spare Patrick. Andrew did not have
much to say. He sat by the stove with his son waiting for a
miracle. Oh Em, I started to cry as I watched Andrew sitting

Cinnamon Sour-Cream Coffee Cake

A classic. Serves 10

Ingredients:
2 sticks sweet butter
2 cups sugar
2 eggs beaten
2 cups flour
1 Tbl. baking powder

1/4 tsp. salt
1 cup sour cream
1 Tbl. vanilla extract
Filling:
3/4 cup sugar
2 cups pecans chopped
1 Tbl. cinnamon
1 tsp. nutmeg
Topping:
1/2 cup flour
1/2 cup brown sugar
1 tsp. cinnamon
Utensils:
bundt pan or 10 inch spring
form pan
mixing bowl

Putting it all together:

1. Spray bundt pan with cooking spray.
2. Cream butter and 2 cups sugar. Add eggs, sour cream, and vanilla.
3. Fold in dry ingredients and stir to blend.
4. In separate bowl, mix remaining 3/4 cup sugar with pecans, cinnamon, and nutmeg.
5. Pour half the batter into bundt pan. Sprinkle filling mixture evenly over top.
6. Pour remaining batter over top.
7. In separate bowl mix 1/2 cup flour, brown sugar, and cinnamon.
8. Sprinkle over top of batter. Bake at 350 degrees for 1 hour or until cake tests done. Cool 15 minutes and serve warm.

To err is human.
To blame it on someone else is humaner.

there with Patrick, believing that his son would survive - - his faith strong. I felt ashamed somehow. As if my heart was steeped in fear while Andrew's was filled with anticipation. Where I was fearing God would forget us, Andrew was waiting for God to answer - - his faith unwavering.

At 7:00 AM Patrick's breathing was so shallow that Andrew picked his listless son from the basket and held him close. He must have thought Patrick was about to slip away. Andrew walked to the kitchen window and looked out at the winter sun rising cold and distant on the horizon. He put his cheek next to Patrick's and in a voice cracking with emotion he asked God to heal his son; to spare him if it was His will.

I pressed my body against Andrew's back, my face against his shoulder, and slowly rubbed his arms in an attempt to comfort both of us. And then suddenly Patrick began to cry, too. It was a weak cry, but it had a hungry ring to it. Andrew and I froze. I have to admit Em, that at that moment my optimism was still frail. And then Patrick cried again — stronger and longer this time. Andrew suggested that I try to feed him.

I sat down in the rocker by the fire. Andrew laid Patrick in my arms and pulled up a kitchen chair in front of me. He rested his hands on my knees and watched as Patrick nursed for the first time, and then fell into a deep restful sleep — both of the them; Patrick in my arms and Andrew with his head on my lap.

I have whispered many prayers of thankfulness for the miracle I witnessed. Patrick is definitely my last baby. I could never go through that again.

Love, Hannah

Tart Lemon Curd

**This is so smooth your tongue will think it's died
and gone to heaven. Great on toast, biscuits or even
pancakes and waffles.**

Makes 2 cups

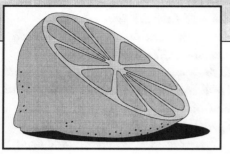

1/2 cup cornstarch
4 egg yolks beaten
1/2 cup fresh lemon juice
3 Tbl. butter

Utensils:
meduim sauce pan
wire whisk
1 qt. crockery or glass jar with
lid

Ingredients:
2 cups sugar
1 1/2 cups water
1/2 tsp. salt

Putting it all together:

1. In sauce pan mix water, sugar, salt and corn starch and whisk until smooth.
2. Heat over medium heat, whisking constantly, until mixture bubbles and is thick and clear.
3. Remove from heat and cool 10 minutes.
4. Whisk eggs into lemon juice and fold into thickened mixture.
5. Return to heat and bring to boil, stirring constantly.
6. Remove from heat again.
7. Add butter and stir gently until butter is melted and mixed thoroughly.
8. Pour into jar and cool. Then cover and store in refrigerator. Lasts about two weeks.

*Face it. Out of the mouths of babes come
words you shouldn't have said in the first place.*

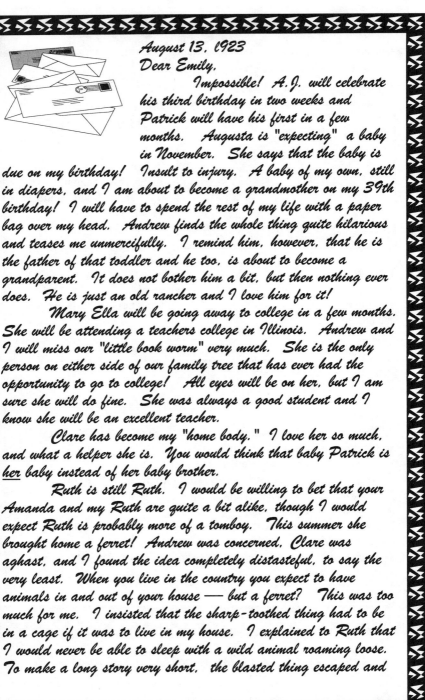

August 13, 1923

Dear Emily,

Impossible! A.J. will celebrate his third birthday in two weeks and Patrick will have his first in a few months. Augusta is "expecting" a baby in November. She says that the baby is due on my birthday! Insult to injury. A baby of my own, still in diapers, and I am about to become a grandmother on my 39th birthday! I will have to spend the rest of my life with a paper bag over my head. Andrew finds the whole thing quite hilarious and teases me unmercifully. I remind him, however, that he is the father of that toddler and he too, is about to become a grandparent. It does not bother him a bit, but then nothing ever does. He is just an old rancher and I love him for it!

Mary Ella will be going away to college in a few months. She will be attending a teachers college in Illinois. Andrew and I will miss our "little book worm" very much. She is the only person on either side of our family tree that has ever had the opportunity to go to college! All eyes will be on her, but I am sure she will do fine. She was always a good student and I know she will be an excellent teacher.

Clare has become my "home body." I love her so much, and what a helper she is. You would think that baby Patrick is her baby instead of her baby brother.

Ruth is still Ruth. I would be willing to bet that your Amanda and my Ruth are quite a bit alike, though I would expect Ruth is probably more of a tomboy. This summer she brought home a ferret! Andrew was concerned, Clare was aghast, and I found the idea completely distasteful, to say the very least. When you live in the country you expect to have animals in and out of your house — but a ferret? This was too much for me. I insisted that the sharp-toothed thing had to be in a cage if it was to live in my house. I explained to Ruth that I would never be able to sleep with a wild animal roaming loose. To make a long story very short, the blasted thing escaped and

Maple Huckleberry Sauce

The best over flapjacks or waffles, but this sauce is also terrific over ice cream, pastry and fresh fruit.

Makes 2 cups

Ingredients:
2 cups fresh or frozen huckleberries (or blueberries)
1 Tbl. lemon juice
1 cup sugar
1 1/2 cups water
1 Tbl. cornstarch
2 Tbl. maple flavoring
dash each: cinnamon, ginger, and nutmeg
1 Tbl. butter

Utensils:
small bowl
medium sauce pan
wire whisk
glass or crockery jar with lid

Putting it all together:

1. Place huckleberries in small bowl and sprinkle with lemon juice, cinnamon, nutmeg and ginger. Toss lightly to mix spices.
2. In sauce pan whisk sugar, water, maple flavoring and cornstarch over medium heat until mixture bubbles and thickens then turns clear.
3. Remove from heat and fold in berry mixture.
4. Add butter and stir to melt.
5. Serve hot or cold.
6. Hide in covered jar in refrigerator.

The bravest person of all was the one who discovered frog legs were edible.

ended up as an unexpected bedfellow with Andrew and me. Chaos ensued. We must have scared the creature half to death because we have seen nothing of it since. I do not rest easy, though. I'm waiting for act two.

Beth has become her father's right hand. She has always preferred to be outdoors. I argued with her for years over cooking, sewing, and housekeeping, but finally gave up. If she wants to be a rancher, let her be a rancher. After all, I believe, to each her own.

What can I say about A.J. and Patrick. In a nutshell? Normal, energetic, and loud.

Good-bye for now, dear Emily. I have bread in the oven and dozens of things left to do before dinner.

Love to all, Hannah

Chicken, Fish & Seafood

October 20, 1923

Dear Hannah,

　　　　Franklin and I were reading in the newspaper this morning about our new president. Franklin calls Mr. Coolidge "milk toast", though I am not so sure. Of course, as with all Presidents, only time will tell. I think we Americans expect too much of our presidents. They are, after all, limited by their "humanness." I will say, however, that Mr. Harding used up every bit of his "human error quotient" as far as I am concerned. I am never happy to see anyone die, but I am pleased to have Warren G. absent away from the White House. Enough! I know how politics bore you.

　　　　I have bigger fish to fry, anyway. There is big news here at the House of Sawyer. Julianna has met a young man, and after what I will call a questionable amount of time, has announced her engagement. His name is Randall Quincy, a seminary student from Atlanta. She met him last summer at the annual church picnic and fell head over heels in love with him. They are planning to marry next fall when Randall completes his seminary training. At least they will have a full year during their engagement to get to know one another. I very much like Randall, and am certain he and Julianna will be very happy together, but these whirlwind courtships these days make me nervous. It seems like young people are in such a hurry to do everything!

　　　　I must close for now, my dear. Franklin and I are expected for dinner at Mother and Father Sawyers. We are leaving a bit early so we can take our time driving. The Fall colors are magnificent this year.

Love, Emily

Curried Chicken Wings

Tangy, but not too hot.
Serves 8

Ingredients:
2 pounds chicken wings
1 cup flour
1 tsp. each: salt, turmeric,
cayenne pepper
1/4 cup olive oil
1 medium onion chopped
1 tsp. curry powder

2 chicken bouillon cubes
3 Tbl. flour
1 1/2 cups water

Utensils:
lg. skillet
lg. baking dish
wire whisk

Putting it all together:
1. Remove sharp tips of chicken wings.
2. Mix together flour, cayenne pepper, salt and turmeric in a paper or plastic bag.

3. Add bouillon cubes to water to dissolve.
4. Shake chicken in flour mix until well coated and brown in olive oil. Discard remaining flour mixture.
5. Lay chicken in baking dish and sprinkle with onion.
6. Over medium heat, to remaining oil in skillet, add 3 Tbl. flour. Stir with wire whisk to blend flour and oil. Slowly add water, and curry and whisk as gravy heats and thickens.
7. Remove from heat when bubbling and pour over chicken. Bake at 325 degrees for 1 1/2 hours.
8. Serve with sauteed mixed veggies.

Misery is a woman with a
live secret and a dead telephone.

December 23, 1923
Dear Emily,

Merry Christmas my dear friend. I hope this Christmas finds you happy and healthy and blessed.

Our lives are busy as usual.

Beth brought home another tiny, motherless kitten to nurse back to health -- a never ending trail of them. This one is a little short haired calico. She has the most vibrant colors and such a sweet disposition and she has wriggled her way into my heart. She follows me everywhere and I suppose I have found myself a new cat. You remember Kitty Moon was nearly twenty when he died four years ago, and I have not had the urge to have another pet after such a long and happy friendship. Of course, we have had a continuous series of barn cats here on the ranch, but none I would have called a friend. However, this kitten is irresistible, and I have named her Faithfully Mine -- Faith for short.

What a holiday season we have had, though raising two young boys requires more energy than did all five of my girls put together. A.J. and Patrick are in uninterrupted motion, and are curious about everything. Last summer, Andrew spoke with A.J. about behaving more like a "big boy" — told him that he should try to be a help to his mother and not cause her extra work. Words I felt were wasted on a three year old, though I admired Andrew for his efforts. A.J. is a child who really does try to please, however, and before I knew it he had filled the bucket in the kitchen sink and was throwing water everywhere. He said he was washing floors. He said, "See, I hepin you Mama." What a mess.

And then there is Patrick, an explosion in waiting, who is just learning to walk. Andrew had to build a fence around the Christmas tree this year to keep Patrick from pulling it over; all those shiny objects were just too tempting.

Back to Beth. She has certainly blossomed into an attractive young woman, confident and capable in every way.

Crab-Stuffed Chicken Breasts

Delightful. The perfect combination of flavors

Serves 12

Ingredients:

12 boneless skinless chicken breast halves washed and dried
1 tsp. each: salt and pepper
The Stuffing:
1/2 cup herb stuffing mix
5 oz canned crab drained
1/2 cup chopped celery
1/2 cup chopped green onion
3 Tbl. butter
3 Tbl. dry white wine
dash of paprika
The Sauce:
1/3 cup grated Swiss cheese
1/3 cup dry white wine
3 Tbl. butter
3 Tbl. flour
1 pint cream

Utensils:

lg. skillet & medium sauce pan
lg. baking dish
toothpicks

Putting it all together:

Butterfly chicken breasts. Sprinkle with salt and pepper.

The Stuffing:

1. Melt butter and toss the remaining stuffing ingredients together. Set aside.
2. Divide stuffing mix among breasts and roll up securing with toothpicks.
4. Place stuffed chicken side by side in well greased baking dish.
5. Bake chicken uncovered for 15 minutes and covered for 30 more at 375 degrees.

The Sauce:

1. Melt butter in sauce pan over low heat. Add flour and whisk to blend. Add remaining sauce ingredients. Cook until cheese is melted.
2. Pour over chicken. Set oven on 325 degrees and warm chicken for 20 minutes. Serve. (Don't forget to remove the toothpicks).

*If at first you succeed —
hide your astonishment.*

She has met a young man and has fallen in love. His name is Richard Stockton. He is from Texas, and Andrew hired him to manage our growing cattle herd. Richard was raised on a family ranch near San Antonio and came to us with much valuable experience and knowledge of livestock. Beth became enamored immediately, though I think at first she was attracted more by his love of animals and intense understanding of them than she was to him personally. I have watched their relationship blossom over the past few months and today Richard asked her father for her hand in marriage. Very old fashioned, but it was clear that Andrew found the gesture honorable and respectful. They are planning to marry some time next year though no date has been set.

Clare too has become interested in a young man. He is Robert Perkins (Rebecca Perkins nephew -- her brother Nathan's boy). How strange it is to see the children of our former classmates becoming romantically attracted to our own, but I do not see this relationship as a very serious one. Clare is young, and she does not seem as mature at her age as my other girls were. She is still painfully shy, but there has always been a tender sweetness about her that makes her fascinating and appealing in a distant sort of way. Robert is gregarious, and boisterous, and shockingly handsome, and he simply adores Clare. He treats her like a fragile prize and I appreciate his gentleness toward her. She finds him entertaining and enjoyable and it is obvious that she is at ease around him -- comfortable in completely being herself.

Mary Ella walked through just now and said to tell you that she is not interested in men. That girl can read over my shoulder faster than I can stop her. Hazardous to my privacy!

Love, Hannah

Chicken and Wild Rice

Tender and moist chicken on a bed of tasty rice.

Serves 8

Ingredients:
1 cooked cup each: wild rice and white rice
1/2 cup chopped onion
1/2 cup butter
3 cups diced chicken
1/4 cup flour
2 cups sliced fresh mushrooms
2 cups chicken broth
1 1/2 cups light cream
1/4 cup sun-dried tomatoes
2 Tbl. parsley
1 1/2 tsp. salt
1/4 tsp. pepper

1/2 cups slivered almonds

Utensils:
lg. skillet
lg. baking dish

Putting it all together:

1. Saute' onion , mushrooms, and chicken in butter until clear. Remove from heat and stir in flour.
2. Gradually add chicken broth, stirring to prevent lumping.
3. Add cream and cook over low heat until thickened.
4. Place rice in greased baking dish.
5. Add remaining ingredients, except almonds, to sauce and pour over rice.
6. Sprinkle with almonds and bake at 350 degrees for 30 minutes.
7. Serve hot. (Tossed salad and biscuits are good companions with this delightful dish).

Children say the funniest things and usually in front of the wrongest people.

May 18, 1926

Dear Hannah,

I am sitting on the verandah at Heartsong, and what memories are my companions! How I love to come here; to remember Aunt Beatrice and to relive the time I spent belonging to this home.

As was her wish Aunt Beatrice willed Heartsong to both My Uncle Edward and my mother! I am sure she did it to force mother to, for once, be nice to Uncle Edward. As it turned out, I was proud of them and their ability to overcome their mutual dislike long enough to deal with the estate. And in the end, they decided that this grand old part of Charleston's history should belong to its residents. A museum it shall be. A monument to the intensity and tenacity of the Southern character. I am glad. It is Aunt Beatrice's legacy. Her determination to save her home; the last shred of what was familiar.

And so now I can come here whenever I like, pay my nickel, and sit on this verandah where I can watch the ships and listen to the gulls, and remember a part of my girlhood. Though Montana has my childhood, and forever my heart, Heartsong represents the butterfly in me; the metamorphosis from child to woman.

I just wanted to share this moment today with you. Truly you alone, my dearest friend, would understand.

Love, Em

Lemon Chicken Saute'

This is easy and quick and a crowd pleaser every time!
<u>Serves 6</u>

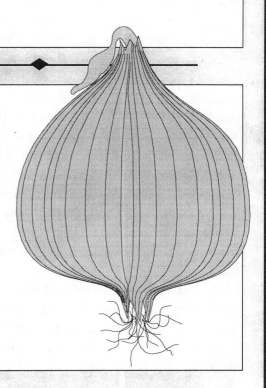

<u>Ingredients:</u>
4 chicken breast halves and 4
chicken thighs skinned
1/2 cup melted butter
1 tsp. crushed garlic
4 green onions sliced
1/2 tsp. thyme
1 lemon peeled and thinly
sliced

<u>Utensils:</u>
lg. skillet
lg. baking dish

<u>Putting it all together:</u>

1. Saute' onions, thyme,
and garlic in butter.
2. Add chicken and
lightly brown.
3. Pour saute' into
baking dish and cover
with lemon slices.
4. Cook uncovered for 1
hour at 350 degrees until
chicken is tender.
5. Serve over rice.

*If you can sleep like a baby —
you don't have one.*

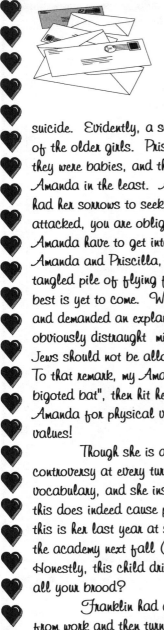

September 8, 1926
Dear Hannah,

Amanda, the boon and bane of my existence, has been expelled from school! It seems as though she, in her typical fashion, has once again managed to commit verbal suicide. Evidently, a school chum was being victimized by several of the older girls. Priscilla and Amanda have been friends since they were babies, and the fact that Priscilla is Jewish never bothered Amanda in the least. As it shouldn't. Priscilla, however, has not had her sorrows to seek, and, I suppose when one's friend is being attacked, you are obliged to take charge of the situation, but did Amanda have to get into a fist fight? It gets worse. It seems that Amanda and Priscilla, along with 5 other girls, ended up in a tangled pile of flying fists and feet. Pay attention, Hannah, the best is yet to come. When the school mistress arrived on the scene and demanded an explanation, all fingers pointed to Priscilla. The obviously distraught mistress made the unfortunate comment that Jews should not be allowed to attend the school in the first place. To that remark, my Amanda shouted, "You are a miserable old bigoted bat", then hit her. Now I am in the position to punish Amanda for physical violence and insolence, yet praise her for her values!

Though she is a very good student she seems to find controversy at every turn. Discretion is not a word found in her vocabulary, and she insists on speaking her mind. Needless to say, this does indeed cause problems from time to time. Thank goodness this is her last year at school. She is sixteen, and will be attending the academy next fall (if her reputation does not precede her). Honestly, this child drives me crazy! How do you ever manage with all your brood?

Franklin had a stern talk with Amanda when he got home from work and then turned to me after she left the room and mused,

Kiwi-Stuffed Rainbow Trout

Deliciously different.
Serves 4.

Ingredients:

2 pound rainbow trout
(cleaned and headless)
1/2 cup butter
1 tsp. garlic powder
24 whole cloves garlic peeled
(trust me here)
4 lg. tangerines peeled and
segmented

4 lg. kiwi peeled and sliced in
thirds
1 lg. onion sliced
1 tsp. salt
1/4 tsp. pepper
1/8 tsp. rosemary

Utensils:

lg. baking dish with cover

Putting it all together:

1. Melt butter and stir in garlic powder, salt, and pepper.
2. Clean and dry trout. Baste cavity with garlic butter.
3. Lay fish in greased baking dish.
4. Stuff fish with one quarter of the kiwi, onion, garlic cloves, and tangerine segments.
5. Pour remaining garlic butter over fish and top with remaining kiwi, tangerines, onion and garlic.
6. Sprinkle with rosemary. Cover and bake at 425 degrees for 20 to 30 minutes. (Do not over cook).
7. Serve steaming hot.

Note: To remove bone from fish: Apply light pressure at spine with sharp knife being careful to only press through meat. Push meat off top side. Then lift tail and gently jiggle fish to remove entire spine. This is easier than it sounds. Go for it!

You can't buy happiness with money
and you can't buy groceries with happiness —
so I guess it all comes out about even.

"I wish she would have blackened the woman's eyes." I dare say my private thoughts were the same, but I am encouraging neither father nor daughter, and the hidden streak of aggression they both foster.

On the lighter side Hannah, Franklin has purchased an automobile. He has been driving all around Charleston as if he were the only man that owned one. I find the contraptions to be noisy things, but they do have advantages over the horse and carriage. He has taken half the neighborhood for a spin in his new machine. Even Maurice was seen being driven through town perched on his master's shoulder. Honestly, people will think Franklin is a lunatic. I am, however, happy to be married to a man who finds such great joy in small things and enjoys every single moment of every single day. I am lucky to love him and have him love me.

My word, that was beginning to sound the slightest bit gushy, and I am sure you are laughing at me by now. I will change the subject once again.

Tell me. How is Babe doing? It is inconceivable that she is married. Is she enjoying California? Is she homesick? Do you miss her dreadfully? I know you must, Hannah. You two were so close even though so different. Send her my love, or better still, send me her address, if you would please, so I may write.

Love, Emily

P.S. Mitchell Rawlins stopped by to see Amanda this evening. I believe the young man has an infatuation for my youngest daughter. How strange it is. Though Amanda is very pretty, most young men can barely keep their eyes off her sister. They are usually endlessly attracted to Julianna's charming personality and gentle manner. Mitchell is different, however, he has never seemed to notice Julianna's loveliness, only Amanda's liveliness. He can visit with her for hours, though in the past their conversation has hardly been

Smoked Salmon and Spinach Pasta

Subtle flavors and ravishing colors.
<u>Serves 6</u>

Ingredients:
2 cups heavy cream
4 Tbl. sweet butter
1 tsp. salt
pinch of nutmeg

1 pound spinach noodles
1 Tbl. grated Parmesan cheese
2 pounds flaked smoked salmon
1/3 cup chopped dill

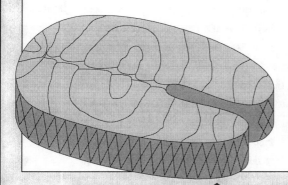

Utensils:
large pot
medium sauce pan
large bowl
pasta tongs

Putting it all together:

1. Simmer cream, nutmeg, salt and half the butter. (Do not boil).
2. Bring 4 qt. salted water to boil in large pot. Start the noodles boiling. (3-4 minutes only!)
3. Add salmon, parmesan and dill to sauce. Remove from heat.
4. Drain pasta and slide into large bowl.
5. Cover with sauce and toss lightly.
6. Serve immediately.
7. Make pigs of yourselves.

Whoever said, "where there's smoke there's fire",
never owned a fireplace.

her for hours, though in the past their conversation has hardly been romantic, since for the most part they talk of airplanes, horses, or boats.

From the first time he saw her, when she was only a child of eleven, he was drawn to her in an innocent way. He was then a young man in his early twenties, and though he has been interested in women his own age, off and on over the past few years, he never seemed serious about any of them.

Now tonight he comes, bringing flowers for my daughter. From where I sit I can see them visiting on the verandah. Something has changed in the way he looks at her, and she at him. It causes my breath to catch in my throat to think that Amanda has grown into a young woman. How can this be the same child that participated in an unladylike brawl just hours ago. I find her to be an enigma.

Young love. Do you remember it Hannah? How it made us tingle with anticipation. I will tell you, Hannah, just between us, sometimes when I look at Franklin I still feel that same tingle.

Em

Shrimp with Apples and Snow Peas

An explosion of unexpected flavors!
<u>Serves 4</u>

Ingredients:
1/2 pound of snow peas
trimmed and stringed
1/2 pound red bell peppers
slivered
1/2 cup butter
2 cups tart apple slices
2 Tbl. brown sugar
1 chopped onion
2 pounds medium shrimp
cleaned and veined
1/4 cup vermouth
2/3 cup Dijon mustard
2 Tbl. corn starch
Utensils:
lg. skillet
lg. pot

Putting it all together:

1. Saute' onion in butter over medium heat until onion turns clear.
2. Add shrimp and toss rapidly for 1 minute.
3. Add cornstarch to vermouth, brown sugar, mustard and mix well.
Then pour over shrimp and toss.
4. Add snow peas and red pepper. Toss again.
5. Cover and simmer 2 minutes.
6 Serve hot over rice. Yikes!

If you really look like the picture on your driver's license, you are definitely not well enough to drive.

May 27, 1927
Dear Emily,

I got a letter from Babe yesterday and Mary Ella the day before and it reminded me that I have been remiss in my own letter writing; you, of course, were first on my list.

Babe's infant son, Loran, is doing well and his sister Angela has become her mother's helper. Did I mention that Clare is expecting in July? This business of becoming a grandmother is difficult to get used to, and I would not be smug about it if I were you Missy Emily -- your turn is coming. My grandchildren call me Nanna, though I am hoping yours will call you Granny!

Mary Ella is doing well at school and will be graduating in June. She is hoping to find a teaching position in Montana -- she misses home so much.

Beth and Richard are doing well. She works right beside him every day and they are raising a fine herd of cattle in Texas, near San Antonio. Richard teases that if she ever learns to cook, he will have married the perfect woman. Beth takes his lighthearted harassments in stride and says he, not she, belongs in the kitchen. It makes her father cringe, but I think Beth and Richard are made for each other.

Ruth has decided to go to linguistics school and then on to the mission field. Yes you heard me. Ruth, my tomboy, my resident savage, who I love dearly, but has made my life a flurry of adventurous events. This, as usual, is her decision. One she made on her own, and I am happy for her. Ruth's faith has truly matured in the past year and I am not surprised that her obsessive nature has taken her in this direction. She, like all the other children, has the fortitude to do anything, and be anything, she wishes -- it simply took her longer to realize it.

A.J. is definitely his father's son -- cut off the same limb. The two of them are off together hunting or fishing whenever Andrew has a chance. The first time they went fishing, Andrew was such a proud papa. He was taking his son out to teach him to fish. Well guess who caught all the fish? And guess who didn't

Scallops in Wine Sauce

Smooth and creamy and seasoned to perfection.
<u>Serves 6</u>

2 cups dry white wine
1/4 cup butter
4 finely chopped shallots
24 finely sliced mushrooms
1 green bell pepper chopped
2 Tbl. minced parsley
2 Tbl. flour
2 to 4 Tbl. heavy cream
6 thick slices of sourdough
bread toasted and buttered

Ingredients:
2 pounds scallops washed and
drained

Utensils:
lg. skillet
warm dinner plates

Putting it all together:

1. Simmer scallops in wine for about 5 minutes. Drain scallops and reserve the liquid.
2. Melt butter and saute' shallots, mushrooms, green pepper and parsley. Stir in flour until blended.
3. Gradually stir in reserved liquid and cream.
4. Add the scallops.
5. Serve hot over sourdough toast.
6. Add a tossed salad and you have a delightful supper.

So I'm fat. You're ugly. I can diet.

get a nibble? Emily, I thought I would die laughing as I eavesdropped from the kitchen window. They were cleaning A. J.'s fish on the back porch and I heard six year old A.J. say to his dad, "Thanks for taking me fishing, Dad. It's really easy, isn't it?"

Raising boys is most certainly not the same as raising girls! A.J. and Patrick are a series of interesting events. Boys, like men, for instance, feel it entirely acceptable to relieve themselves outdoors wherever convenient and inconspicuous – – one of the benefits of being male I suppose. And, they have some very descriptive and unacceptable words to summarize this process! Recently I overheard A.J. telling Patrick, who is now five, that it's a good idea to do this deed on thistles and other weeds. I suppose A.J. felt it would somehow be a natural weed killer. Who knows! Well, last week we were invited to the McCleary's for dinner. They have two boys, nearly the same ages as ours, and a daughter, Evangeline, who is three. Ethan and Elliot are nine and eight, respectively. They like to play with our boys, and the four of them seem to get along pretty well.

When dinner was ready Margaret sent Rudyard out to get the boys. He found his two sons and A.J. right away, then asked about Patrick. A.J. mentioned that he had seen Patrick go behind the barn. When Rudyard rounded the corner of the barn he startled poor Patrick who was standing there watering a patch of thistles. Patrick got a bit flustered and stuttered, "I-I-I-I'm just thissing on your pistles, Mr. McCleary." Rudyard said he nearly chewed a hole in his cheek trying not to laugh. He sent Patrick off to the house for dinner, and then later, when the children were not present, repeated the story. Andrew and Rudyard seized up with laughter, but I think we are raising another generation of cheeky men.

Aren't you glad you have girls?!

Love, Hannah

Beef, Pork & Wild Game

March 30, 1928

Dear Hannah,
　　Amanda's wedding was pleasantly
uneventful. What a relief. I never know what
will happen from one moment to the next with
that girl. I have to admit that she was the prettiest bride I have ever
seen. Her ivory colored dress shocked everyone but me. After all, I
raised this headstrong creature. She just could not be persuaded into
white, no matter what I said. I can't really blame her. She looks
simply "dead" in white. That red hair and white skin were never meant to
be wrapped in something so colorless. She was magnificent in ivory
and walked down the aisle on her father's arm with an air that dared
anyone to defy her. Sound familiar? Her Mitchell thought she was
dazzling, as did her father.

　　The fact that Mitchell Rawlins is 13 years Amanda's senior
bothered Franklin a bit at first, but I felt that Amanda needed a
mature man. After all, let's face it, a younger man might have been
trampled by her indomitable spirit; the very thing Mitchell adores in her.
George Rawlins, of course, declared loudly that he felt Franklin's
daughter had made a fine choice. Franklin in turn, reminded George
that Maurice was now an in-law!

　　Amanda and Mitchell will be staying right here in Charleston.
Mitchell opened an aviation charter, cargo, and maintenance service
here after the war, and it has blossomed into a thriving business. He
also offers instruction and Amanda has pleaded with him for months
to teach her to fly. Her father is horrified by the thought, but I am
secretly envious. Think of it Hannah. To soar like the gulls over the
sea has been a life long fantasy; a fantasy that my daughter may
realize!

　　As for Julianna, Randall accepted a post in a church in
Philadelphia and he and Julianna moved there in May. I am sure they
will love it. Philadelphia is such a beautiful city; so full of history
and culture. She has been a wonderful companion; more like a

Best Beef Stroganoff

Tender bits of beef smothered in mushroom sauce.

Serves 8

1 garlic clove minced
3 Tbl. butter
3 Tbl. flour
1 Tbl. tomato paste
3 cups beef bouillon
1/2 tsp. salt
1 cup cream
2 Tbl. sherry
1 cup sour cream
1 tsp. parsely
1 pound egg noodles

Ingredients:
1 pound beef sirloin cut
against the grain into 1/4 X 1
inch pieces
1/4 cup olive oil
1 cup sliced fresh mushrooms
1/2 cup chopped onion

Utensils:
lg. skillet
lg. baking dish

Putting it all together:
1. Brown meat quickly with olive oil in a hot skillet. Remove to baking dish and set aside.
2. In skillet, reduce heat and, to remaining oil, add mushrooms, onions, garlic. Cook until onion is clear.
3. Spoon into baking dish.
4. Back in the skillet, melt butter. Add flour salt and tomato paste. Stir in beef bouillon and cook until slightly thickened, stirring constantly.
5. Pour into baking dish. Stir to mix ingredients.
6. Bake at 350 degrees for 30 minutes until meat is tender.
7. Remove frm oven and add sherry, cream, and sour cream.
8. Boil noodles and drain. Pour meat mixture over top. Sprinkle with parsley.

I'm so far behind, I think I'm first.

friend than a daughter. I will miss Julianna, but she has a right to her own life in any place she chooses, and I am confident that happiness and serenity will follow her.

Yesterday as I watched Amanda pack her things I suddenly realized that our house was being emptied of our offspring; children grown and starting families of their own. Just Franklin and me again. Like it was in the beginning. Strangely, I find it both comforting and disconcerting.

With Love, Emily

Braised Beef Fajitas

Spicy South of the border flavors.
<u>Serves 6</u>

Ingredients:
1 1/2 pounds round steak quartered
1/2 cup tequila
1/2 cup fresh lime juice
3-4 cloves garlic minced
1 tsp. salt
1/2 tsp. black pepper
1 sm. onion thinly sliced into rings
1 Tbl. olive oil
1 green bell pepper sliced into strips
12 flour tortillas warmed

Condiments:
Guacomole, Salsa, Sour Cream

Utensils:
lg. skillet (cast iron is best)
broiling pan
lg. baking dish

Putting it all together:
1. Place beef in baking dish. Mix together tequila, lime juice, garlic, salt and pepper and pour over meat. Cover tightly and refrigerate for overnight.
2. In skillet, saute' onion in oil for 2 minutes. Add peppers and cook 2 more minutes.
3. Drain marinade from beef and discard. (The juice, not the beef!).
4. Broil meat at medium heat 3-4 minutes per side.
5. Carve meat (against grain) into thin strips.
6. Quickly stir meat and veggies together in skillet and cook for 2 minutes or until well heated.
7. Fill tortillas and add condiments as desired.

I gave up smoking, drinking and sex.
It was the worst hour of my life.

August 11, 1928

Dear Emily,

　　　Boys will be boys! At least that is what Andrew believes should gloss over a variety of minor sins. I am comforted only in that Margaret's boys are equally energetic and mischievously creative as our own.

　　　I don't know if I ever mentioned to you that Margaret is a large woman. Large might be a bit of an understatement, though her size does not seem to limit her in the least. She is so energetic and jolly and full of fun that one hardly notices her size. At least I did not, but the boys -- hers and mine -- found a pair of her bloomer-like winter under garments to be just the right apparatus for parachuting off the roof! Unfortunately, Patrick, who is the youngest of the four boys, was encouraged to be the first jumper. Doctor Torgeson set his broken leg and poor Patrick will spend the remainder of the summer on crutches. Honestly, that child. I doubt he will live to see ten.

　　　Andrew was angry about the incident and decided that all four boys were far too idle -- like your mother used to say, "Idle hands are the devil's workshop" -- what a terrible expression! Anyway, Andrew, with Rudyard's full support, has educated the three older boys, Ethan, A.J. and Elliot on the benefits of hard work. They will spend the rest of their summer building a diversion dam on Calliope Creek that will be used to irrigate Andrew's expanded hay fields. I agreed whole heartedly, but Margaret, soft hearted as she is, found it necessary to sneak the boys treats while they worked.

　　　I will admit that the beginnings of this project were frustrating for the boys. Though the creek is narrow and barely a trickle this time of year, the boys had trouble

112

Beef Brisket in Garlic au Jus

Tender "cut with your fork" beef in tasty juice.
<u>Serves 8</u>

Ingredients:
4 pound brisket
2 Tbl. garlic powder
2 Tbl. onion powder
2 tsp. salt
1 tsp. pepper
1 cup water
1 cup red wine

1 lg. onion thick sliced
4 cloves crushed garlic

Utensils:
bulb baster
medium roaster with lid and
interior rack
lg. platter

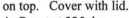

Putting it all together:

1. Mix together seasonings and rub into meat.
2. Pour liquid into bottom of roaster, to make au jus, and center the rack.
3. Place brisket in roaster on rack. Dot with garlic and place onions on top. Cover with lid.

4. Roast at 325 degrees for 3 hours covered.
5. Remove lid and roast at 375 degrees for an additional hour, BASTING, THOROUGHLY, EVERY 10 MINUTES.
6. Remove from roaster and slice against the grain.
7. Serve brisket on platter covered with au jus.
8. This is wonderful with roasted potatoes and baby carrots!

*One way to save face is
to keep the lower half shut.*

getting the foundation of their dam to hold -- water undermining their work and all. They complained to Margaret and her sense of fair play. And so when Andrew and Rudyard went to check on the boy's progress they found Margaret sitting in the creek, her size corralling the creek behind her while the boys busily worked on their project downstream. Neither man had much to say as they walked away, though they did comment that Margaret had picked a good hot day for a dip.

Love to all,

Hannah

Old-fashioned Meatloaf

An all time family favorite
Serves 8

Ingredients:
2 pounds extra lean ground
beef
1 cup tomato sauce
2 eggs

1 cup milk
2 cups bread crumbs
1 tsp. salt
1/2 tsp. pepper
1 tsp. basil
1 tsp. thyme
1 tsp. parsley
2 gloves garlic crushed
1 small onion finely minced

Utensils:
lg. bowl
lg. loaf pan
2 freshly scrubbed hands

Putting it all together:

1. In bowl, place all the ingredients (except 1/2 the tomato sauce) and mix well . (I have tried lots of ways to do this but the very best way is to use your hands. Get in there and squish everything together thoroughly! Pretend you're a kid. This can be fun.)

2. When all the ingredients are thoroughly "squished", pat mixture into well greased loaf pan. Cover with remaining tomato sauce and bake at 375 degrees for about 1 hour or until meat pulls away from sides of pan and has crispy edges.

3. This is my best friend's absolute favorite dish. When she comes to dinner, I serve it with mashed potatoes, buttered peas and buttermilk biscuits with honey. Whoever said, "food isn't love" just doesn't get it!

The cost of living is high
but consider the alternatives.

July 30, 1929

Dear Hannah,

We had the loveliest spring this year, but southern summer has definitely reared its ugly head! It has been hot, sticky, and suffocating every day for over two weeks! This kind of weather is hard on all of us, but especially Leona. Her stroke last fall left her partially paralyzed, and it has affected her speech so badly that she simply refuses to talk at all. Poor old dear. I never thought I would miss her voice, but now that I do not hear it at all, I feel strangely deprived (or depraved depending on how you look at it). I spend long hours in her room reading to her and writing letters for her. I can honestly say that I have grown to genuinely love the old biddy, and she me.

Julianna and Randall have been home for a visit these past two weeks. Last evening Amanda and Mitchell came for supper, and it was wonderful to have my family all sitting around the dinner table together once again. Randall is quite a musician and had brought along his mandolin. After supper the young people went out onto the verandah to enjoy what cool the evening could provide. Randall proceeded to play several secular songs, while Julianna sang along with that marvelous soprano voice of hers. Soon Amanda joined in, and then Franklin. Mitchell does not sing very well, but he does play the harmonica. They were all singing together, improvising harmony as they went along. The sound of their voices was sweet in the stillness of the evening. Leona's bedroom is at the far corner of the house with the window facing the avenue and a sidelong view of the verandah. When I entered her room, I could tell that she was straining to listen to the goings-on outside, so I positioned her at the window where she could see the verandah. I sat down beside her. We listened to the music and I hummed along quietly to myself. Either the songster's moods changed, or they ran out of silly songs to sing, because it got very quiet for a few

Pork Tenderloin in Mustard Sauce

Sweet succulant pork in a tangy sauce.
Serves 8

The sauce:
1 cup hot and spicy mustard
1/4 cup seasoned rice vinegar
1 cup white wine

Utensils:
lg. roaster with lid
lg. platter

Ingredients:
4 pound pork tenderloin
1 qt. sauerkraut

Putting it all together:

1. Pour sauerkraut, including juice, into bottom of roaster.
2. Place tenderloin on top of sauerkraut.
3. Mix the mustard, vinegar, and wine together and pour over meat.
4. Cover and roast at 325 degrees for 4 hours.
5. Remove from roaster and slice into 8 pieces.
6. Spoon out sauerkraut onto platter. Arrange pork on top and serve hot.

Warning: The aroma of this dish cooking will lure everyone into the kitchen hours before dinner is ready. Carry a gun.

Remember:
When you are over the hill, you pick up speed.

minutes. Then Randall and Mitchell began to play *Amazing Grace*, my most favorite of all hymns. Soon my family's voices, blended in harmony, filled the night. Leona reached for my hand and squeezed. I will remember forever the look of perfect peace on her stroke ravaged face. What a brave old soul she is.

I was reminded of you today when I realized that it was nearly huckleberry season. I get homesick every summer at this time, even after all these many years. How I miss you and our Montana. Pay no attention to my melancholy tone. I actually think the happiest thoughts when I reminisce. I have had many blessings in my life, and have nothing to regret. It is only that I believe we are a part of our environment; what is familiar as a child becomes what is the norm, and everything else, no matter how charmed, is second best. I have often wondered if heaven would be in Montana!

Enough for now.
Hugs and kisses to all of yours. Emily

P.S. I am "expecting" to become a *Granny*. Julianna made the announcement over supper. And we are all thrilled. She is due in December.

Sweet 'n Sour Pork Ribs

You can never cook enough of these.
<u>Serves 4 (maybe)</u>

<u>*Ingredients:*</u>
2 pounds pork ribs
1 cup catsup
3/4 cup brown sugar
1/2 cup vinegar
3/4 cup water
2 Tbl. worcestershire sauce
1/2 tsp. chili powder

1 small minced onion
1/2 tsp. each: salt and pepper

<u>*Utensils:*</u>
broiler pan
lg. baking dish

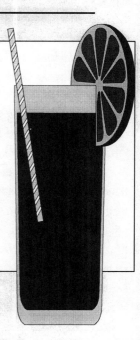

<u>*Putting it all together:*</u>

1. In broiler, brown ribs.
2. Place ribs in baking dish.
3. Mix together remaining ingredients and pour over ribs.
4. Bake at 250 degrees for 3 hours uncovered.
5. Serve hot with green salad and biscuits. Chocolate cake might be good too!

When in doubt mumble.

November 12, 1929

Dear Hannah,

     I am writing with yet another birthday wish. How can you look forward to this celebration of aging, while I feel like gravity is tugging at parts of me that I never before noticed. Nonetheless, I hope your birthday is blessed with the happiest memories.

     Oh, Hannah, last month's stock market debacle has had a horrendous effect on the East and South. We are just beginning to realize the magnitude of this economic disaster. The papers have reported suicides, murders, personal devastation, and the most unbelievable financial ruin. Fortunately for us, Franklin never believed in the stock market and instead invested more wisely in other areas. We have no debt, and though we lost a considerable amount of cash when the bank failed, we are far from destitute.

     As for you in Montana, I feel you will not realize the breadth of this disaster for many months, but I am more than relieved that you also own your property and stock and I am hoping you have little debt. Franklin says we will all face a long recovery.

     Julianna's baby is due in just three weeks and I am so excited, though the poor girl has had the worst pregnancy. She has been so sick and I am sure she is more than ready for this baby to be born.

     As for Amanda. She finally convinced Mitchell to teach her to fly, and has indeed learned to do so. She has passed all her requirements and yesterday Franklin and I were at the airfield to watch her do what they call "solo" (that is flying all by herself!) Franklin's heart was in his throat, but my soul soared with her, exhilarated at the mere vision of flight. She, of course, did marvelously well, and we all celebrated with champagne glasses filled with cider afterwards. (This prohibition!)

     Later, Amanda privately suggested that I go flying with her this afternoon. I did not tell Franklin, since he would have certainly been unwilling for me to go, and you know how I hate to disobey him.

Cajun Lamb Chops

These are best done outside on the grill.

<u>Serves 4</u>

<u>*Ingredients:*</u>
8 loin lamb chops 1 1/2 inches
thick
2 tsp. cayenne pepper
1 tsp. black pepper
1 tsp. white pepper
1/2 tsp. garlic powder
1 tsp. dry mustard
2 tsp. onion powder
1 tsp. salt
1 tsp. dried thyme
2 Tbl. butter melted mixed
with 2 Tbl. lime juice

<u>*Utensils:*</u>
small bowl
barbecue grill or broiler

<u>*Putting it all together:*</u>

1. Brush chops with butter and lime juice.
2. In a small bowl mix remaining ingredients.
3. Press mixture to both sides of chops patting each chop to adhere spices.
4. Barbecue on high heat for 1-2 minutes each side.
5. Serve hot with cold applesauce on the side.

I'm so broke I can't even afford to pay attention.

Instead, I simply met Amanda at the airfield shortly after lunch. She fastened me tightly into the seat in front of her, and gave me a few brief instructions, while she searched my face for apprehension. There was none, I assure you. I had dreamed of this moment for years. How could I be anything but enthused!

Though I was dressed warmly and the day was not very cold, the brisk wind on my face as we sped down the airfield caused me to gulp my breaths. And then I felt the plane leave the ground and surge upward into the sky. The earth fell away at the same time the clouds drew near, and I literally screamed with ecstatic abandon; a scream that sounded almost primal, Hannah, deep, pent-up up, and shameless. I felt fabulously free. I waved my arms above my head screaming and screaming with absolute delight. Amanda laughed; enjoying my pleasure.

We soared in wide spiraling circles over a familiar, though miniature, Charleston and its harbor dotted with tiny ships. Low over the sea we flew, parallel with the gulls I had envied so often. "Look at me, now!" I shouted to them when we came close. "Look at me, now!"

We flew over Heartsong, flying directly toward it from the ocean. I had the incredible sensation that I was holding still, while it was rushing out to meet me. The sight of it from above was thrilling. The sight of it all was thrilling, and when we rolled to a stop back on the airfield I was utterly speechless, overwhelmed. I pressed my face into my hands and wept happy tears of jubilation. Something I had anticipated and fantasized about for so long had come to pass, and I was consumed with emotion.

Franklin nearly fainted when I told him what I had done. For a moment I thought he would be furious, but instead he held me close and asked, What is it like to be a bird, my dear, daring, Emily?"

Someday, Hannah, you will be a bird as well.

Love, Em

Andrew's Vension Mincemeat

Makes the best mincemeat pie you can imagine
<u>Makes 8 pints</u>

Ingredients:
3 lbs. ground deer meat
2 cups sugar
2 cups brown sugar
1 stick butter
1 pint apple cider vinegar
1 tsp. ground glove
1 tsp. cinnamon
1 tsp. mace
1 tsp. nutmeg
1 tsp. ginger

1 tsp. black pepper
1 cup applesauce
2 tart chopped apples
2 cups raisins
2 cups dates chopped

Utensils:
lg. pot
8 pint canning jars
or 1 gallon freezer bags

Putting it all together:

1. Brown meat in butter.
2. Add remaining ingredients and simmer to reduce liquid, stirring often. (Mixture should be thick.)
3. Freeze in freezer bags or can in pint jars.

Middle age: When a broad mind
and a narrow waist change places.

March 3, 1930
Dear Emily,

Surely you must be teasing me. Flying? A dream come true indeed. I would have never thought you so brave, but then you always were full of surprises. How excited I am for you. I am imagining that before I know it you will be flying your own plane. I will telegram Miss Earheart immediately, to inform Amelia about her aviation competition. Can Amanda fly you here!?

Calving season is nearly upon us and I am more than ready for the newness of spring. This winter has seemed endless, and need I remind you how I feel about March. But like you say, "March is the promise of spring." La-de-da.

You will never guess who is running for the State Senate. Yes ma'am, the one and only Winslow Parish. Winslow and Eleanor moved to Helena shortly after they were married and he has practiced law there for years. They have four daughters who are very close together in age -- Yvette, Annette, Colette, and Georgette -- Eleanor's idea, naturally. She said she wanted names that sounded French? Brother. Anyway, these four young ladies are all gorgeous like their mother, but they have personalities just like Winslow. Can you imagine living in a house filled with Winslows? A frightening thought indeed! However, the obvious point, is of course, that life would be much worse had they looked like him , and acted like her. Forgive me. I am off the track and besides I am sounding catty.

Rudyard says Winslow is running on a very good platform and that he feels Mr. Parrish will make a "darn fine senator." I wish Winslow the very best of luck. If nothing more, the Senate, with Winslow in attendance, will certainly not have a dull moment. He has gotten to be pretty polished these days, Em; his gregarious nature has turned shrewdly diplomatic. Andrew says Winslow is such a smooth talker that he could "tie his shoe laces with his tongue."

Orange Quail and Wild Rice

Delicious! <u>**Serves 4**</u>

Ingredients:
4 whole quail dressed
juice of one orange
1/2 tsp. garlic powder
1/2 tsp. onion powder
1 tsp. rosemary
1 tsp. thyme
1 tsp. salt
1/2 tsp. pepper
1 Tbl. butter melted
2 cups white rice cooked
2 cups wild rice cooked
1 garlic clove crushed

1 tsp. orange zest
1/4 tsp. salt
pinch of parsley

Putting it all together:

1. Toss white and wild rice with orange zest, crushed garlic, 1/2 tsp. salt and parsley.
2. In small bowl mix juice and remaining seasonings.
3. Baste birds with juice mixture.
4. Stuff birds with rice mixture and place on roaster.
5. Roast at 350 degrees for 30 minutes, turning once and basting once more with juice mixture.
6. Baste with half the melted butter and continue roasting for 15 minutes more.
7. Serve with steamed veggies and fresh bread.

Never loan money to a friend —
it ruins their memory.

My Grandbaby population is continuing to grow Em, and I have taken to plucking at my gray hairs. Andrew says I will soon be bald. How lucky you are that you have that strawberry hair -- gray does not show as easily. Not that you would ever admit to having any.

Back to my grandbabies. In case you have lost count, Clare has three boys, Beth has a boy and a girl, Babe has a boy and a girl and one on the way. Ruth says she will never be bothered with marriage and Mary Ella does not like to discuss it. They must get their independent streak from their father.

Speaking of grandbabies. Do remember to give Julianna the crocheted booties and jacket I have enclosed for her beautiful baby boy. Brewster Franklin Quincy is quite a big name for a little man, don't you think? Maybe she will just call him "Brew."

Love, Hannah

Antelope Steaks in Mushroom Sauce

Seconds? Yes please!
<u>Serves 4</u>

Ingredients:
The Antelope:
4 antelope steaks 1/2 inch
thick boned and tenderized
1/2 pound bacon
1 cup mushrooms sliced
1 lg. onion chopped
1/2 cup flour
1 tsp. garlic salt
1/2 tsp. pepper
1/4 cup butter
The marinade:
1 cup red wine

4 cloves garlic crushed
dash each salt and pepper
The sauce:
2 cups fresh mushrooms whole
1/2 cup sour cream
2 cups milk
1 Tbl. Parmesan cheese
1 tsp. garlic powder
1 tsp. onion powder

Utensils:
medium sauce pan
lg. skillet

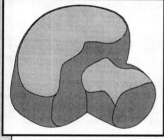

Putting it all together:
1. Mix marinade ingredients and cover
steaks. Refrigerate over night. 2.
Remove steaks from marinade, (discard
marinade) pat steaks dry and cover with 2
cups milk. Soak for 30 minutes.
3. In skillet, fry bacon, mushrooms, and
onion. Remove from grease and set aside.
4. Pull steaks from milk and dredge in dry mix made from flour,
garlic, salt and pepper. Then fry in bacon grease until tender.
5. In bowl, blend milk, sour cream,Parmesan, garlic powder and
onion powder. Pour over steaks and simmer 2 minutes.
6. Serve hot with roasted potatoes.

Time wounds all heels.

127

September 21, 1930

Dear Hannah,

Greetings to you on this glorious first day of Fall. I will get right to the point. Let us address this gray hair business! Let me assure you that not a single living soul will ever see a gray hair on my head. I have no intention of growing old gracefully and intend to fight it to the very end. You will find me lying in my casket with reddish blond hair. Or perhaps I will be bald, as well. Let me tell you what I did to myself.

I was fussing about my hair. It was looking dull and the slightest hue of silver could be discerned. Ever helpful Amanda suggested we color it. What a terrible mess. I prefer to find green in my wardrobe rather than in my hair, thank you very much Amanda! Amanda found the whole thing hilarious, Franklin was aghast, and I am mortified. The cat won't even look at me, for heaven sakes! Amanda said she would be back in the morning to "fix it," whatever that means. Thank goodness I look good in hats.

Besides my green hair, I find that my arms are not long enough to read the newspaper. Franklin sweetly suggested that perhaps I may be needing spectacles. What next! I suppose it will be my hearing.

Poor Franklin is the one who is actually getting hard of hearing. It seems as though everything I say has a different meaning to him, and it can be utterly comical. For instance, last night I asked if he would get me a glass of water, and he brought me a fly swatter! We both laughed ourselves sick.

Let me continue. We had planned a picnic for today. Franklin thought we should ride out to see the reservoir made by the new diversion dam. It was several miles to the dam and even though the weather looked foreboding we decided to go ahead with our plans. We got into the automobile and rode along as the weather deteriorated all around us. By the time we reached our destination it was truly miserable; cold and windy and generally disagreeable. Dear sweet Franklin. He never fails to see the good in everything, and today

Chili Con-Moosey

Yikes - this is good!
<u>Serves 6</u>

Ingredients:

2 pounds moose meat cut into
1 inch pieces
1/4 cup olive oil
1 cup onions chopped
6 cloves garlic crushed
6 cups water
1 cup green bell peppers
chopped
2 tsp. chili powder
1/2 tsp. turmeric
1 tsp. cumin

1 tsp. worcestershire sauce
2 tsp. sugar
3 tsp. salt
10 oz. stewed tomatoes with
juice
2 cups kidney beans
2 qts. water
1 Tbl. salt

Utensils:

lg. soup pot

Putting it all together:

1. Soak beans over night in 2 qts.
water and 1 Tbl. salt. Drain and set
aside.
2. In soup pot, brown meat with
onion and garlic in olive oil.
3. Add 6 cups water and remaining
ingredients including beans, and
bring to boil. Simmer 3 hours.
4. Serve in large bowls with
cornbread and honey on the side.

A bachelor's idea of gourmet:
Anything above room temperature.

was no exception. How I wish I was equally gifted.

We sat for awhile looking out the window at the lake and the weather. Or rather, I was looking at the weather and Franklin was admiring the lake.

And then he asked," Emily, don't you think it's a nice little lake they've made?"

And I said, " I think it looks a little foreboding if you ask me."

And he replied, "Well don't you think it's a little cold for boating?"

Amanda says we should go to Hollywood and become another *Burns and Allen!*

Our love to all your family. Happy tenth birthday to A.J. Ahh youth!

Love, Emily

Elk Steak Burgers and Onions

This is quick and easy!
<u>Serves 4</u>

1/4 cup applesauce
1 lg. onion sliced thick
4 potatoes quartered
1/4 cup olive oil
2 Tbl. soy sauce
4 large sesame seed rolls

Ingredients:
2 pounds ground Elk
1 egg
1 tsp. garlic powder
1/4 tsp. pepper

Utensils:
lg. bowl
lg. skillet
2 freshly scrubbed hands

Putting it all together:

1. In bowl, mix, Elk, egg, garlic powder, applesauce and pepper. (mix with hands). Form into four large patties 1 inch thick.
2. Coat skillet with olive oil.
3. Place patties in skillet surrounded by potatoes and covered with onions.
4. Drizzle with soy sauce.
5. Fry on low heat 7 minutes on each side or until potatoes are tender and meat is done.
6. Serve meat and onions on toasted and buttered sesame rolls with potatoes on side.
Note: There won't be room for Jello.

Where does virgin wool come from?
From sheep who run the fastest.

July 4, 1931
Dear Emily,

Ruth left for Kenya today. It gives a totally new meaning to "Independence Day." Andrew and I put her on the train to New York this morning and I had the sickening feeling that I would never see her again. I know that I can be melodramatic, but Emily — Kenya! Actually, Africa needs Ruth. If nothing else the children in the missionary school will learn to laugh and they certainly will never be bored. Isn't this the girl that had to be dragged to church every Sunday? And isn't this the same teenager that said, "There is no God!"? Well she must have changed her mind, or God changed it for her. Let me tell you something, Emily. That blond, gorgeous, 25 year old that I put on the train this morning, believes in God! Her face was the vision of peace and her resolve never stronger. I still remember the day she sat with me at the kitchen table and told me about her decision to become a missionary. I thought, anyone but Ruth, though God knows our hearts better than we do. Bless you as you go, my dear Ruth. God will be by your side as He has always been by mine.

Clare is happy in her new home. I am so glad she and Robert decided to stay in Montana. Why is it that the rest of you find it necessary to move to the ends of the world? You, Emily, in South Carolina, Babe in San Francisco, Beth in Texas, and now, Ruth to Africa. Thank goodness Mary Ella is finally coming home. She has taken a teaching position in a small town near here. Just a one room school house but I'm sure she will be happy.

We are still struggling to keep hold of the ranch. The boys are a big help to Andrew even though they are still pretty young. It seems like we just get through one financial crisis and another is scratching at the back door. But we will survive. It will take a lot more than the depression to push us off our land. We are in a lot better shape than most. It's so sad to see people losing everything they have ever worked for.

Potpourri

A.J. and Patrick are growing like weeds. A.J. is quiet like his Dad and Patrick is happy go lucky, always looking on the bright side.

Beth and Richard are going to stay in San Antonio. They are, after all, better off there. Richard's ranch is on family land and he will not have to worry about losing it. Beth loves Texas and I know she is happy. I miss her, but she has to live her own life; just like she always has.

As for Andrew and me, it's funny, we have never had less money, but on the other hand, we have never been happier. It has been years since we actually worked side by side and we are really enjoying each other. It doesn't seem possible that we have been married thirty years. You know Emily, I was looking at him the other day, and he is actually better looking now than he was when we got married. I wish I could say the same for me. Why is it that men get better looking as they get older and women just get older? It doesn't seem fair does it? Why am I asking you? I can't even get you to admit that you ever reached thirty. You vain thing.

Oh, I almost forgot to tell you! Douglas Farthington has moved back here and I must say he has gotten better with age. Not only is he still strikingly handsome but he has changed considerably, Em. Gone is the arrogance and self involvement. Though I did not want to, I find that I like him very much. He took over the family ranch when his dad died last spring, and he has bought the adjacent ranch which, of course, is Second Wind. It is comforting somehow to know that Douglas owns the place where I was raised and where my papa is buried.

We had Douglas over to dinner Sunday after church and he had the boys, especially A.J., on the edge of their chairs with stories of all the places he has been. He was a mining engineer and traveled all over the world with his work. Really an interesting fellow.

All for now.

Love from all of us, Hannah

Cheesey Chicken Enchiladas

Creamy and delicious!
Serves 4

Ingredients:
2 cups diced cooked chicken
4 oz. canned green chiles
7 oz. green chili salsa
1/2 tsp. salt
2 cups whipping cream
12 corn tortillas
1 1/2 cup shredded jack cheese

Utensils:
11 X 13 baking dish

Putting it all together:

1. Combine chicken, green chiles, and salsa.
2. Combine salt and cream.
3. Do these one at a time: Soften tortilla in oil, dip in cream and fill with chicken mixture and roll up. Place rolled tortilla in baking dish.
4. When all tortillas are in baking dish, cover with cream and top with cheese.
5. Bake at 350 degrees for 25 minutes.
6. Serve hot.

*If everything is coming your way,
you're in the wrong lane.*

October 9, 1931

Dear Hannah,

It's funny how the passage of time heals old wounds. I had not thought of Douglas for years and now he is back in Bluebird. You and your "convenient amnesia!" Don't try and fool me Hannah, you were as sweet on Douglas Farthington as I was. For that matter, all the girls were. And by the way, I still haven't forgiven you for the "Huckleberry Cobbler" incident. Don't play dumb. You always said that you had nothing to do with it, but I know better. There isn't another person on earth devious enough to think up such a terrible plot. Why I ever trusted you to make that donation to the church baked goods auction for me I will never know. What a hateful thing to do .... using 2 cups of salt in place of 2 cups of sugar. Now thirty-five years later, I want to know how you arranged for Douglas to buy that infamous cobbler! Remember how it was? The person that <u>made the dessert</u> had to share it with the person who <u>bought the</u> dessert. My cheeks flush at the mere memory. The look on his face! You miserable wretch ..... I could have killed you. When I told Franklin the "cobbler story" at supper tonight he nearly laughed himself into convulsions. And then there was the time at the Harvest Festival Dance. You stole the last bloom of the season off my mother's prize winning rose bush. The last time I saw that rose was in your teeth as you glided across the dance floor doing some silly imitation with Andrew. I still can't believe you told mother that I picked that yellow rose and gave it to you! You are a scoundrel!

There is no real news to tell here. Franklin's business is surviving the depression, just barely. I have cut corners until there aren't any more to cut. And we are just "making do" with everything we can. We are doing without everything but happiness. Franklin, Mr. Sunshine, always has something positive to say and refuses to be depressed (forgive the pun.) Bless his heart. He says to tell you that he is "finer than frog's hair." Really.

Good-bye for now, dear. I'll write again soon.

Love, Emily

Classic Mac and Cheese

A classic Indeed.
Serves 6

Ingredients:
6 cups cooked macaroni
3 Tbl. butter
1 Tbl. flour
1 tsp. salt
dash pepper
3 cups milk
2 cups shredded sharp
cheddar cheese

Utensils:
lg. baking dish
medium sauce pan
wire whisk

Putting it all together:

1. In sauce pan melt butter over low heat and stir in flour, salt, and pepper.
2. When mixture bubbles, gradually add milk ,whisking constantly.
3. Continue to whisk until mixture begins to bubble. Do not boil.
4. Remove from heat and add 3/4 of the cheese.
5. Spoon macaroni into baking dish and cover with cheese sauce and top with remaining cheese.
6. Bake at 375 degrees to heat thoroughly.
7. Serve hot.

*A woman's place is in the home,
and she should go there directly from work.*

August 9, 1933
Dear Em,

I was thinking today that I am in my fiftieth year — fifty years old on my next birthday! I imagine that you, no doubt, still think you are some sort of spring chicken. One half of a century, Emily. I am betting that you are really dreading your fiftieth birthday next July. Be consoled. Fifty is only significant when you are forty-nine!

We have had a tremendous summer. The apple and pear trees have never been heavier with fruit, the garden produced and produced until I could hardly keep up with it, and it seemed like the barnyard came alive with baby "everything" this year. Even my old, nasty tempered sow, Pork Chop, had 14 piglets! Thinking of that pig reminds me to tell you about our almost unfortunate "Chase Race" last Sunday.

Clare, Robert and the boys were over for Sunday dinner. I guess it was about 3:00 when all the commotion started. The adults were sitting on the porch enjoying the afternoon. Robby was playing with the dog, and supposedly watching Davey, who just turned three in July. I was totally engrossed in a story that Andrew was telling, when all of a sudden we heard a crash, a scream, and a squeal. The sound had come from the barn so we jumped up and rounded the east side of the house just in time to see Davey running as fast as his chubby little legs could carry him with Pork Chop right behind him, gaining ground with every step. My heart stopped! Robert was off the porch first, running to intercept child and pig, and he managed to grab Davey just ahead of Pork Chop. Well, let me tell you Emily, it took an hour before we all caught our breath, Davey calmed down, and the pig was securely back in her pen. Then Andrew took the child up onto his lap to ask him what had happened. Davey had evidently been teasing Pork Chop and her babies. I guess Pork Chop figured enough was enough, and just came right through the pen after him. The rest is history, but Davey's explanation of

138

The Mother of Spaghetti Sauce

Rich and thick and meaty.
<u>Serves 8</u>

Ingredients:

1 pound lean ground beef
1 pound ground Italian
sausage
1/4 cup olive oil
1 large onion chopped
5 cloves of garlic crushed
1 green pepper chopped
1 Tbl. worcestershire sauce

10 oz. can of tomato sauce
10 oz. can of stewed tomatoes
6 oz. can tomato paste
2 Tbl. Italian seasoning
1 cup grated Parmesan cheese

Utensils:

lg. soup pot

Putting it all together:

1. In soup pot, brown meats, onion, garlic and green pepper in olive oil. Drain excess oil.
2. Add remaining ingredients and simmer for 1 hour, stirring often.
3. Remove from heat and refrigerate over night.
4. Re-heat and simmer for 1 hour.
5. Serve over pasta and top with fresh Parmesan.

*The three day weekend
was created because it's impossible to cram all
the bad weather into two days.*

how "pig chased boy" is the best. Davey said, "Well, Grandpa, I said blah blah piggy, and then she said blah blah Davey and then here she come." Kids. How they ever manage to live long enough to grow up is a mystery to me.

I got a wonderful letter from Ruth last week. She just loves Kenya. There are 37 students in the missionary school now and she is really enjoying teaching. The way she describes the country side, you would think it was paradise, though the thought of living so near dangerous animals and snakes does bother her some. But all in all she manages pretty well. She doesn't sound the least bit homesick. It appears Ruth has found her niche in life. I'm truly happy for her, but I miss her terribly.

Babe's new baby girl sounds just precious. How I wish I could see her, but the odds that I will ever be able to travel to San Francisco are just about zero .... it might as well be Mars. You know what she named her? Emily Kay! Don't get a puffed head.

Well, my dear, I must close for now. My love to all.

Hannah

Sweet and smooth.
Serves 8

Ingredients:
1 cup each in bite sized
chunks: fresh pineapple,
cantaloupe, seedless grapes,
plums, honeydew, raisins
2 Tbl. Grand Mariner liqueur
1 Tbl. Amaretto liqueur
dash of lemon juice

Utensils:
"scooped out" pineapple or
prettiest glass bowl

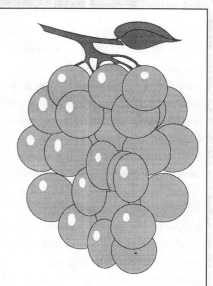

Putting it all together:

1. Toss all ingredients together and marinate for two hours in
refrigerator.
2. Serve on chilled salad plates.

*A youthful figure is what you get
when you ask a woman her age.*

April 18, 1936

Dearest Emily,

Would you like to hear some good news? My darling Mary Ella is to be married on the 10th of September. I thought she would never do it. After all, she was thirty-three last April. She always said that teaching was her life, and her students her children. I guess she wasn't planning on Stewart Parker waltzing into her happily exclusive world and sweeping her off her feet. He is a widower with three beautiful children that just adore Mary Ella, I might add. The way he looks at her, Em! You would think she was the only woman in the world! I'm sure she will be gloriously happy.

Doc Torgeson regretfully retired this past month. He and Madge are moving to Nevada — hoping for milder winters I suspect. It makes me sad to see him go. He has been such a big part of our lives — delivered all but two of our children, and over the years, patched all our hurts. I was remembering the first day I met him. It was Thanksgiving when I was only fourteen! It seems like a million years ago. We had a big send off party for Doc and Madge last Sunday, and Doc introduced his new replacement. His name is Lucas Winkler. Such a handsome young man fresh out of medical school. His name rang a bell and sure enough I find that he is the son of Rev. Winkler. Poor Pastor Winkler only lasted here at our little country church for a year. He really belonged in the city and I heard through the grapevine that he was happier at his new church in Denver. Well it seems that Lucas found Montana country living more attractive than his father did, and here he is.

No more news, and I must rush off as I am expecting guests for dinner.

Lovingly, Hannah

Hot Curried Fruit

Great with Ham or Pork.
Serves 8

Ingredients:
1 cup each canned fruit:
pineapple chunks, apricots,
peaches, pears, and mandarin
oranges
1/2 cup maraschino cherries
1 cup brown sugar
1/4 tsp. salt

1 Tbl. curry powder
1/2 cup butter

Utensils:
lg. sauce pan
baking dish

Putting it all together:

1. In sauce pan combine brown sugar,
salt, curry powder and butter and bring to
boil.
2. Simmer 5 minutes.
3. Place fruit in buttered baking dish.
4. Pour sauce over fruit.
5. Bake at 300 degrees for 20
minutes.
6. Cool slightly and
serve warm. Yum!

Alimony: Bounty from the mutiny.

August 28, 1936

Dear Hannah,

This has been a busy and emotional year for me, Hannah. I was just sitting here by the fire wondering what else could possibly happen in the Sawyer household in 1936.

I miss Leona, Hannah. She taught me so very much over the years; especially patience, toward the end. She suffered for such a long time and she never really complained. If I loved her for nothing else, it was for that lesson.

My life is changing so rapidly that it makes my head spin, and you know that change has never been easy for me. Is the world moving faster or is it my imagination?

The depression has certainly left its mark among our friends and neighbors. Who would have ever thought that something like this could happen in a great country like ours. But then I suppose nations are like people, and they are allowed their ups and downs too. Speaking of depression, I certainly sound like I am in one as I re-read this letter. I was thinking the other day that I am still, after all these years, homesick for Montana. Isn't that the silliest thing? After all, I am "you know what!" But then, it wouldn't matter how old I was, the memory of the everlasting youth and freshness of Montana will always be a part of me.

My Amanda is going to have a baby in January, but this pregnancy has not slowed her down in the least. She is so strong and healthy and refuses to behave like a mother-to-be. I teasingly asked Mitchell to please get control of his wife and he said he wouldn't want to. He says he likes her just like she is. I have to agree. For all her uncivilized behavior, she still is a huge measure of joy in my life.

Love to Andrew and the boys.

Missing you, Emily

Parmesan Veggie Saute'

Serve this as a compliment to any main dish.
Serves 6

Ingredients:
4 carrots slivered
12 green beans trimmed and
stemmed
1 each red and yellow bell .
peppers cleaned, seeds
removed, and sliced in length
wise eighths
1/2 cup sun-dried tomatoes
1 cup fresh mushrooms
3 green onions sliced
1/4 cup peanut oil

1 cup chicken broth cool
3 Tbl. soy sauce
1 tsp. honey
1 tsp. cornstarch
1 tsp. herb vinegar
1/4 tsp. rosemary
1/4 tsp. tarragon
1 Tbl. Parmesan cheese

Utensils:
wok
flat wooden spoon

Putting it all together:
1. Heat oil in wok and saute' onions and carrots 3 minutes.
2. Add beans and tomatoes and continue to saute' for 3 more minutes.
3. Add mushrooms and peppers and saute' for 3 *more* minutes.
4. Mix broth, soy sauce, honey, vinegar and spices together.
5. Stir cornstarch into broth mixture until smooth.
6. Pour immediately over veggies and toss lightly to thoroughly coat. Sprinkle on cheese.
7. Sauce will thicken and clear.
8. Serve hot over fried rice.
9. Don't forget the chop sticks.

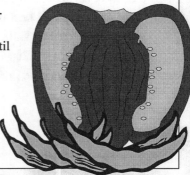

The light at the end of the tunnel is a train.

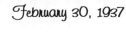

February 30, 1937

Dear Hannah,

Granny here! Yes Amanda has had her babies; plural, as in twins! Identical boys, Spencer and Nicholas. She is doing fine as are the boys. She already has her figure back and is once again running around like a mad woman. She just packs up the boys and goes! Her father told Amanda that if he caught her with those babies in an airplane he would strangle her! She just laughs at him. I am not worried. Mitchell would put his foot down to that, I assure you.

The twins are handsome lads, Hannah. Dark like Mitchell, with Amanda's eyes. We are all so proud. Julianna's wonderful little Brewster is almost seven, and I was ready for more babies in my life. Julianna brought Brewster, and came for a visit as soon as she heard Amanda had delivered her babies. So here I am surrounded by my daughters and grandchildren. I couldn't be happier.

Brewster is a sweet child, and such a natural comic. I had told him once when he was being crabby that he should put a spring in his step, a song in his heart and a smile on his face. Well, yesterday when I was having not the best of days, he said, "Granny you should put a song in your step, a smile in your heart, and spring in your face!"

Good-bye my dear. Tell Mary Ella that her Auntie Em hopes she has the very happiest future with her new family.

With Love,
Emily

Eastern Herb Fried Rice

**This is wonderful stuff and
it goes with just about everything.**
<u>**Serves 8**</u>

Ingredients:

1/4 cup sesame oil
3 green onions sliced
1/2 cup chopped shitake
mushrooms
1 clove garlic crushed
1/4 tsp. turmeric
dash nutmeg
dash pepper
4 cups cooked and cooled

white rice
1/2 cup bacon cooked crispy
and patted dry & crumbled
1/4 cup soy sauce

Utensils:

wok
flat wooden spoon

Putting it all together:

1. Heat oil in wok.
2. Saute' next six ingredients for 5 minutes.
3. Add rice and bacon and toss in hot wok until rice begins to crisp.
4. Add soy and toss to blend.
5. Remove from heat and serve.

Note: I like to put the wok right on the table in its wooden stand. Rice will stay hot much longer.

He who hesitates is interrupted!

October 2, 1939
Dear Emily,

    Don't be such a worry wart, Em. A. J. will be fine! He is just another one of the Hansen children with infectious wanderlust.

    A. J. was never meant to be a rancher, or a farmer, or a "stay at home" anything. I am convinced that he was born with a head full of far away places. And even though it breaks my heart to see him leave, the navy was really his only choice. There is no future here for a young man like A. J., looking for adventure. Emily, I learned a long time ago that to try and confine my children in the name of protection is a cruel love indeed. He goes with my blessing and, I must admit, my heartache. But without my blessing his heart would ache, and I love him too much for that.

    Patrick is seventeen! Can you believe it? What a handsome young man he is. He looks so much like my father that sometimes the resemblance literally stuns me. He is still a happy-go-lucky character with a hilarious sense of humor. He simply cripples me with laughter regularly. He loves living here on the ranch. He doesn't particularly like ranching, but the country surroundings seem essential to him. He notices everything — every detail of every animal — the progress of every flower. Nothing escapes his keen eye, and what a joy he is. He has developed a friendship with young Dr. Winkler, and has taken an interest in medicine. I suppose this should not surprise me, Patrick certainly has the intelligence to tackle such a career, but who knows what notions travel through a teenager's mind -- thoughts here today and gone tomorrow.

    How are Amanda's babies doing? Twin boys; poetic justice if you ask me! I would bet that she is a wonderful mother, however; so full of life and energy. She will enjoy those babies like no one else possibly could.

    Good-bye for now, my dear friend. Give my love to Franklin.
Love, Hannah

Spicy Mexican Rice

It's what goes with all your Southwestern dishes!
<u>Serves 6</u>

Ingredients:

2 Tbl. oil
1 cup uncooked rice
14 oz. stewed tomatoes
1 small onion minced
1/4 cup green pepper chopped
2 tsp. salt
1 tsp. chili powder
1 tsp. cumin
2 cups water

Utensils:
lg. covered skillet

Putting it all together:

1. In large skillet, heat oil and add rice.
2. Saute', stirring for 5 minutes or until evenly browned.
3. Add all ingredients and mix well.
4. Cover with lid and simmer until rice is tender and moisture is absorbed. (approx. 20 minutes)
5. Remove lid and allow to dry out a bit.
6. Serve warm.

I don't believe in drinking in front of the children, and when they aren't around who needs it?

January 28, 1940

Dear Hannah,

I am writing with bad news. Franklin has had a mild heart attack. The doctors do not seem to be overly concerned, though they do insist that he retire immediately. He is forbidden any unnecessary physical activity or excitement. Franklin has always been such an active man that this sudden immobilization would be devastating. For that reason he has decided to continue living, at top speed, like he always has.

I was hysterical over this decision at first, but then Franklin took me by the hand and walked me out onto the verandah. We sat in the swing that he gave me so many years ago and he poured out his inner most thoughts, fears and desires. His life has been so very full. If he could live it all over again, he would change nothing; not one single moment. He wants to live the remainder of his life surrounded by laughter and newness. He wants to swim with his grandsons, argue with his daughter, take long walks with me, and continue to run his business. If his life is shorter because of this, he is ready to accept it.

As for me, I have shed many tears. The thought of life without him terrifies me, but I am adopting your philosophy, Hannah. To confine him in the name of protection would indeed be a cruel love. For that reason, I will thank God for every day that is allowed my husband.

Love, Emily

Fettuccine Verde'

Bring an appetite!
<u>**Serves 4**</u>

Ingredients:

8 oz. green fettuccine noodles
6 Tbl. butter
1 cup green onions minced
2 garlic cloves minced
1 cup whipping cream
1/2 cup Parmesan cheese,
freshly grated
dash nutmeg
salt and pepper to taste
Parmesan cheese for topping

Utensils:
lg skillet

Putting it all together:

1. Boil noodles according to package directions and drain well.
2. Melt butter in skillet and add onions and garlic.
3. Cook, stirring, two minutes.
4. Add cream and cheese and simmer.
5. Add noodles and tosss to coat.
6. Add spices and serve immediately topped with cheese.

Note: I like to eat this with a large spoon and a fork. Makes the eating more fun!

A dog's life isn't so bad — all he has to worry about is the toilet seat falling on his head.

September 13, 1940

Dear Hannah,

Hannah, have you heard? Roosevelt has announced that he is running for a third term.

Franklin says that he is sure such an act is unconstitutional, but I think he is simply wanting a change. Roosevelt's New Deal and all his new politics have indeed caused change, but in what direction I am not sure, and I find him very controversial.

As for me I am more worried about Europe heating up for war once again. I am recognizing the same patterns and events that sent us into a world war twenty years ago. The shipyard is a beehive of activity and cloaked in secrecy, and I am afraid. I feel the threat of war oppressively hovering over us.

I worry about your A.J. and my Mitchell serving in the military so far from home, and what I perceive as safety. What if war *did* break-out? I am horrified by the thought. Forgive me, Hannah. I am muttering onto the paper, and did not intend to write about my fears.

On the lighter side Franklin's health seems to be steadily improving. His color is good and he does not seem as breathless. If I could just get him to rest more I would be a happier woman. Did I say lighter side? It appears that my fears have overshadowed any hope of that today.

I will write again when I can communicate in a happier fashion.

Love, Emily

Artichoke Tomato Bake

Ever so easy.
Serves 6

1/2 tsp. sugar
1 tsp. salt
1 tsp. pepper
1 tsp. thyme
1 tsp. basil
14 oz. can artichoke hearts
quartered
4 medium sized tomatoes
thickly sliced
2 Tbl. butter melted

Ingredients:
1/4 cup butter
1 large onion chopped
3 cups fresh bread crumbs

Utensils:
lg. skillet
lg. baking dish

Putting it all together:

1. Fry onion in butter until transparent.
2. Mix in bread crumbs, sugar, salt, pepper, thyme and basil.
3. Remove from heat.
4. Butter baking dish and fill with alternate layers of artichokes, tomatoes, bread crumb mixture, ending with bread crumbs.
5. Drizzle butter over top.
6. Bake at 350 degrees for 45 minutes.
7. Serve hot.

The only people who hear both sides of an argument are the neighbors.

October 8, 1940

Dear Emily,

For heaven's sakes, Emily dear, get hold of yourself! If there is one thing I have learned in my fifty-six years it is that I cannot control the events in my own backyard, let alone the ones threatening the world. Yes, I too fear the death of my loved ones, the death of our American way, the death of freedom , but you must remember my dear, darling, wonderfully tender, Emily that God makes no mistakes. Whatever happens is within an omnipotent plan. I pray for A.J. and Mitchell every single day, and yes I have fretful times, but I have to believe that no matter what happens, God has a plan. Be strong in that knowledge, Em.

I have watched the last of my baby birds leave the nest. Patrick has gone to Missoula — to the university and eventually on to medical school. I will miss him, not only because he is the last to go, but because he has been such a bright spot in my life. I thought the other day how I regretted my being pregnant again at the age of thirty-seven, but as I looked at him leaving in his coat and tie — so handsome, and intelligent, and clever, and wholesome in a manly sort of way — I thanked God for being smarter than me, and allowing my precious Patrick to become a warm fuzzy nugget of love in my life.

I will tell you what, Emily, dear. Let us, you and I, make a pact - - like we did when we were children, and could not in any way control the events of our lives. Repeat after me: I promise to be strong for you and you for me. I promise to hold my head up, and face whatever is my lot with courage found deep in my being. I promise to remember to be thankful every day for what I have, and what I do not have. And, I promise to remember to tell the ones I love that I do indeed love them.

All right. Let's get busy.

I love you! Hannah

Cheddar Gratin Spuds

Creamy and cheesey potatoes.
Serves 4

Ingredients:
2 pounds red-skinned potatoes
washed and trimmed
1 cup ricotta cheese
3/4 cup chopped parsley
2 tsp. salt
1 tsp. pepper
dash nutmeg
1 egg beaten
1-2 cups cream
3/4 pound sharp cheddar
cheese

Utensils:
large pot

large baking dish
medium bowl

Putting it all together:

1. Into large pot, thin slice potatoes and boil in salted water for one minute. Remove from heat and drain.
2. In medium bowl, combine ricotta and parsley and seasonings.
3. Add cream mixed with egg and cheese.
4. Butter baking dish and layer with half the potatoes.
5. Cover with half the sauce.
6. Repeat.
7. Bake at 350 degrees for 35 minutes until sauce bubbles, but do not boil.
8. Cool 10 minutes and serve warm. Wonderful!

*If your outgo exceeds your income,
then your upkeep will be your downfall.*

June 25, 1941

Dear Hannah,

Franklin and I had been out picking peaches all day long and we were a sticky mess by the time we got home. Peaches are like huckleberries, only bigger, and I cannot seem to pick them without eating them; so sweet and juicy and yummy. Franklin is just as bad!

I filled the bathtub with scented salts, and was looking forward to a long leisurely soak, but made the mistake of leaving the bathroom long enough to get a ribbon to tie up my hair. When I came back I found that long legged Franklin lounging in my tub! Of all the nerve. And then he proceeded to make some extremely suggestive remarks about men and women and bathtubs. He thought he was very smart, and I threatened to pour my glass of iced tea over is head if he did not immediately remove himself from my bathroom. He told me I wouldn't dare, but when I tried to make good on my threat he grabbed my wrist and pulled me into the tub, bathrobe and all! That man! I am hoping you live with a male that is not clinically insane! Don't you dare repeat this story, Hannah Marie. I should not have told you.

We are having a summer of unbearable heat. Amanda, Spencer, and Nicholas spend a good share of their time at the shore playing in the water, and the boys are brown as bears. They are four and half now, and as wild as March Hares; poetic justice indeed. Amanda, however, does not find their energy level extreme, and thoroughly enjoys their antics.

I went with them to the beach last week. It was a particularly stifling day, and I was refreshed by the breeze offered up by the sea. We girls waded while the boys swam, then later, rested in the shade of my big beach umbrella while the boys played in the sand. Amanda had packed a picnic lunch, and in the wide assortment of foods were some hard boiled eggs. If I had to pick a more mischievous twin it would be Spencer, though what Spencer doesn't think of Nicholas does. The trouble began when Amanda gave each one a hard boiled egg. The boys

Broccoli Swiss Quiche

Yes real men *do* eat this!
<u>Serves 8</u>

Ingredients:
1 10 inch unbaked pie shell
(Use Hannah's Perfect Pie
Crust in dessert section)
1 small onion chopped
1/4 pound bacon
4 eggs beaten
1 cup milk
1 cup

cream
1 cup chopped broccoli
1 cup shredded Swiss cheese
pinch each: cayenne pepper,
salt and tarragon (ouch!)

Utensils:
10 inch pie plate

Putting it all together:
1. Fry onion and bacon together until bacon is crispy. Drain well.
2. Lay broccoli in bottom of pie crust. Cover with bacon mixture.
3. Mix together eggs, milk, cream and seasonings.
4. Gently pour over top.
5. Cover with cheese and bake at 425 degrees for 15 minutes.
Reduce heat to 300 degrees and bake an additional 40 minutes or until
center is firm.
6. Let cool 5 minutes. Serve warm with tossed salad and huckleberry
muffins.

I finally got it all together
and now I can't remember where I put it.

are in the barbaric habit off cracking boiled egg shells open on one
another's foreheads, amid much laughter and cavorting. Well today,
Spencer had obviously anticipated this uncivilized ritual and tucked a
raw egg into the picnic basket before they left home. While Amanda and
I were visiting, I absently noticed Spencer return the egg Amanda had
given him and choose another. Nicholas ran up to Spencer and proceeded
to happily crack his egg on his brother's forehead. Unfortunately for
Nicholas, Spencer did the same. Raw egg ran down a shocked Nicholas'
face. He stood there in stunned silence for a moment, and then the fight
was on. Raw egg and sand mixed together is a most unpleasant
combination, as you can imagine. What a horrible mess smeared over
both boys. Amanda was trying hard to be stern as she separated the
twins and lectured them on good sportsmanship and brotherly love, though
I knew she was ready to burst into laughter at any moment. And then all
three of them did start laughing, which led to rolling around in the sand
again. Honestly, Hannah, the whole thing was very funny, but I am
afraid my daughter is raising a pair of savages!

Love, Emily

Odds and Ends

Making seasoned vinegars, salsa and homemade mayo.

3 Seasoned Vinegars:
Ingredients:
3 qt. bottles with corks
3 qts. white vinegar
3 sets of herbs to fill 3 bottles
    Bottle #1. lavender and mint
    Bottle #2. tarragon, sage and
summer savory
*Wash herbs and arrange in
bottles. Fill with vinegar and
let stand two weeks. Use on
everything from salad to fruit.*

*Each time you use vinegar
replenish bottle with vinegar.*
Bottle #3. 1 cup fresh or
frozen raspberries, cinnamon
stick, and vanilla bean
*Mash berries and cover with 1
qt. vinegar. Let stand over
night. Strain and discard
raspberry pulp. Place vanilla
and cinnamon in bottle and fill
with raspberry vinegar.*
These last about 6 months!

Homemade Mayo: 4 cups
Ingredients:
3 eggs
1 Tbl. Dijon mustard
1/2 tsp. salt
dash pepper
1/4 cup fresh lemon juice
2 cups quality vegetable oil

In blender, on medium speed,
mix all ingredients except oil
for one minute. With blender
still running, slowly dribble oil
into mix until all oil is
included. Mix will thicken
and turn creamy white. Store
in refrigerator.

Fresh Salsa: 2 cups
Ingredients:
2 lg. peeled tomatoes chopped
4 tomatillos chopped
2 each fresh Anaheim &
jalapeno chiles seeded and
chopped
1 tsp. each: cumin, sugar, lime
juice, and minced cilantro.
dash salt and pepper.

**Mix all ingredients together.
Refrigerate two hours.
Yikes! Serve with warmed
tortilla chips.**

The Lord giveth and the government taketh away.

Christmas 1941

Dear Emily,

My Christmas wish this year is for a world at peace, and that somewhere in the future I will be able to say that my son did not have to die in vain. The shock of A.J.'s death is still as cold as the icy wind of winter. My only refuge is the knowledge that he died being where he wanted to be, doing what he wanted to do, and being whom he was, a young man looking for adventure.

A.J. had sent me a picture of himself and several of his Navy buddies enjoying the surf and each other -- in this place he called "paradise." As I studied the picture, I envied my son's good fortune to be able to visit such an exotic place. Little did I know that a week after that picture was taken, all those young men would be dead. The Navy regrets that they were not able to recover the body of my son.

Oh Emily, I pray for all the mothers who lost their sons, all the wives who lost their husbands, and all the children who will never know their fathers. It is unbelievable that America is at war once again.

Andrew, is inconsolable. I have watched this man march through life taking whatever was his lot with dignity and determination. But A.J.'s death has taken the spark completely out of him. He is drained -- emotionally bankrupt, and I pray every day that God will heal his broken heart. I wish there was a way for me to take him away from here for awhile. Remove him from the memories.

The rest of the family is dealing with their loss as best they can, but the death of a sibling is too great -- a dismemberment.

As for me, there are days that run into the next, and my grief is beyond what I think I can bear. I am depending on my own advice, however, and believe beyond a shadow of doubt that in time I will heal.

Loving you, Hannah

Desserts
&
Candies

February 17, 1942

Dearest Hannah,

My heart goes out to you. No one really knows how you must feel, but know that I love you and I am here, always, if you need me. I promise to be strong for you, as you have always been for me.

Pearl Harbor is a disaster that will remain forever a scar on this country, as it will the hearts of those that lost loved ones. God be with you and Andrew, Hannah. We will all pray for peace.

Love,
Emily and Franklin

Forever Chocolate Cake

Deliciously decadent— to die for!
Makes 10 inch cake

Ingredients:
3 cups flour
1/2 cup unsweetened cocoa
1/2 tsp. baking powder
1 tsp. salt
1 cup vegetable oil
1/2 cup butter
3 cups sugar
5 eggs
1 1/4 cups milk
1 cup grated semi-sweet chocolate
1 tsp. vanilla

The filling: Yes!
8 oz. cream cheese
1 egg
1/2 cup sugar
1/2 tsp. almond extract
1 cup semi-sweet chocolate chips

Utensils:
mixing bowl and mixer
10 inch spring form pan

Putting it all together:
1. Whip filling ingredients (except chocolate chips) together until fluffy. Fold in chocolate chips and set aside.

Cake Batter:

2. Sift all dry ingredients together and set aside.

3. In mixing bowl beat butter, oil, sugar, vanilla and eggs for five minutes at high speed.

4. Reduce speed & gradually add flour mixture alternately with milk.

5. Fold in grated chocolate.

6. Spray spring form pan thoroughly with cooking spray. Spoon half the batter into bundt pan and shake gently to distribute evenly.

8. Drop in dollop of filling evenly around cake batter.

9. Cover with remaining cake batter. Bake at 350 degrees for 30 minutes and 325 degrees for 30 more or until cake rises fully and top begins to separate. Cool 15 minutes and turn out on cake plate. Cool completely, then drizzle cake with hot fudge just before serving.Wow!

*If it's true that money talks —
mine just said "bye-bye".*

April 5, 1944

Dear Hannah,

I have been sitting here in the garden re-reading your letters from the past few months and I am relieved as I notice that you are gradually beginning to feel stronger. I can hear it in the way you turn a phrase and the barest hint of that old sarcastic humor is peeking through the pages. Your last letter was as welcome as the flowers in May and afford me a much needed laugh. How good it is to hear your written voice with its old spark evident again. I really laughed at your story about Mabel Priddis and Lem Wollan's engagement. Imagine them marrying so late in life. Are they really 81 and 83? And did he really tell everybody at the picnic that they had to get married?! But the funniest part is you being so surprised by his announcement that you spit punch out all over Andrew. You always did have a problem with self-control, Hannah. And yes, I agree. You will indeed be wearing a paper bag over your head for a while to hide your embarrassment

So you think you are the only one that can make a fool of yourself. Not so. The following lesson in humility should only be shared with someone who truly appreciates the human ability to make a fool of ones self — and who enjoys a good laugh. Therefore, I am sharing this with you!

Picture, if you will, a "slightly" over weight, "slightly" over 50, woman in her bath robe, at 7:00 A.M. on a Saturday morning. Now picture, if you will, a cat stuck in a tree bawling as if she were being murdered (the cat, incidentally, was given to the woman by her youngest daughter). And picture the tree, located at the edge of the front yard next to the sidewalk. If the picture is clear, then you will have no trouble imagining 6 neighbors and 2 firemen trying to get the woman out of the tree long after the cat has scampered down of its own accord. Franklin laughed. In fact, the entire neighborhood is laughing. <u>Now</u> who is wearing a paper bag over her head? You are the last person from whom I would expect empathy, so I know you

Spiced Pumpkin Cheesecake

The grand finale to any dinner.
<u>Makes one 10 inch cheesecake</u>

<u>Ingredients:</u>
The crust:
1 cup crushed ginger snaps
3 Tbl. melted butter
1 tsp. cinnamon
2 Tbl. brown sugar

The filling:
4 - 8 oz. packages cream
cheese softened
1 1/2 cups sugar
5 eggs
1/4 cup flour
2 Tbl. pumpkin pie spice
14 oz. can pumpkin
2 Tbl. light rum
1 cup whipping cream
whipped

<u>Utensils:</u>
mixing bowl and mixer
10 inch spring form pan

<u>Putting it all together:</u>
1. Combine crust ingredients and press into bottom of greased spring form pan. Pat firm and chill. Pre-heat oven to 325 degrees.
2. Whip cream cheese and cream till fluffy. Gradually beat in sugar. Add eggs one at a time, beating well after each addition.
3. Gradually beat in flour, spices, pumpkin and rum.
4. Pour batter over crust and bake for 1 1/2 hours. Turn off oven and let cheese cake remain in oven with door closed for another 20 minutes or until filling is set. Cool completely then chill. Remove spring from metal "ring" and serve.

*There is one advantage to being married —
you can't make a fool of yourself
without knowing it.*

165

are laughing too.

All is well here except for this miserable rationing. My "victory garden" has not been much of a victory. This horrible war! Isn't anyone going to stop that maniac! My heart aches for you, and so many people like you, who have lost loved ones in this chaos. I pray every day that today will be the last day of the war.

I got a lovely letter from Julianna last week. She says that she has been active with the USO in Philadelphia and is quite enjoying it. She and Randall are doing fine. Philadelphia is really "home" for them now. They have made lots of friends, and all the activities that go along with pastoring a church keeps them busy. Brewster has become quite an accomplished pianist, and has won many competitions.

I must go for now. Franklin and I are going picnicking and fishing this afternoon at our favorite spot and I am excited to go. George Rawlins said, today at church, that the bass are big and biting! Franklin is all ready to go and I haven't even started to pack our lunch. He will be waiting. (My delightful little garden offered me two worm-eaten tomatoes to take along, but I declined.)

Love,
Emily

Meg's Super Moist Carrot Cake

This cake isn't about carrots!
<u>Makes one large layer cake</u>

Ingredients:
3 cups flour
3 cups sugar
1 tsp. salt
1 Tbl. baking soda
1 Tbl. ground cinnamon
1 tsp. nutmeg
dash ginger
1 1/2 cups corn oil
4 large eggs beaten
1 Tbl. vanilla extract
1 tsp. almond extract
1 1/2 cups walnuts chopped

1 1/2 cups shredded coconut
1 1/3 cups carrot puree
3/4 cup crushed pineapple
The Frosting:
At room temperature: 8 oz.
cream cheese and 6 Tbl. butter
3 cups powdered sugar
1 tsp. vanilla
juice of one lemon
Utensils:
mixing bowl and mixer
2 - 9 X 9 inch square cake
pans (I like glass)

Putting it all together:
1. Sift dry ingredients together.
2. Add oil, eggs, and extracts.   Beat well.
3. Fold in remaining ingredients and pour into well greased pans.
4. Bake at 350 degrees for 50 minutes. (Baking one pan at a time works best unless you have two ovens.) Cool completely, refrigerate 2 hours and frost.
The frosting:
1. Whip all ingredients until fluffy. Place one cake on cake plate. Cover cake with 1/3 of the frosting. Place second cake on top and frost top and sides with remaining frosting. Cut into 2 inch squares and serve.

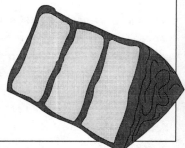

When a man puts his foot down,
it usually means his wife has finished
vacuuming under his chair.

May 7, 1944
Dear Emily,

Patrick was home for Easter and we had a delightful visit. I am thankful that the leg he broke so badly as a child has kept him out of the army. Unpatriotic of me, I realize, but I am not willing to sacrifice another son to this war. He is doing very well at school and truly has his eyes fixed on the medical profession. Unfortunately for Patrick, so does Evangeline.

I suppose Patrick has always loved her. I'm sure that I have mentioned her to you several times. Evangeline is Margaret's daughter. She is eighteen now and Patrick, I guess, simply assumed that she would wait for him while he was at school. She didn't. She announced her engagement to Lucas Winkler in last week's newspaper. I like Evangeline very much and I do feel Patrick took an awful lot for granted — expecting a young girl to read his mind — and him leaving with so much unspoken. But nonetheless she broke his heart. It is so strange that I never noticed how vulnerable he was, and how easily shattered. Young love can be painful, and though I feel for him, I know there is a special girl somewhere out there waiting for him.

After Patrick left today I did something most unusual. While Andrew was off to town I took the day for myself. I packed a light lunch and walked for hours in the woods behind the house. Perhaps I was feeling a bit melancholy, perhaps feeling Patrick's disappointment, and just needed sometime to myself.

How I love this old ranch. So many memories here — Louis and Meg and all of us — Teddy, Augie and Kitty Moon — Toulouse and Tilly. I have lived forty three years here at Calliope Spring. Is it possible? Years, like water rushing by.

I climbed to the very top of the very highest hill and looked down onto the house and out over the ranch. I felt like a queen surveying her kingdom (or should that be queendom.)

Orange Poppy-Seed Pound Cake

You'll need permission from your cardiologist for this one.

<u>Makes one 10 inch bundt cake</u>

<u>Ingredients:</u>
The cake:
1/4 cup poppy seeds
1/2 cup orange juice
1/2 pound butter softened
5 eggs
2 cups sugar
2 Tbl. orange zest
2 cups flour

1 tsp. vanilla extract
1 tsp. almond extract
The glaze:
1/2 cup orange juice
1/2 cup white sugar
<u>Utensils:</u>
10 inch bundt pan
mixing bowl and mixer
small sauce pan

<u>Putting it all together:</u>

1. Soak poppy seeds in orange juice overnight.
2. Cream butter and sugar and add eggs gradually. Beat until fluffy.
3. Add extracts, orange zest, poppy seed and orange juice mixture and mix well.
4. Fold in flour until well blended.
5. Pour into well greased bundt pan and bake at 350 degrees for 50 minutes or until cake tests done.
6. Let cool for 30 minutes. Turn out onto cake plate. Prick holes in top of cake with fork and glaze.

The glaze:
1. Combine in small sauce pan and simmer 5 minutes until light syrup forms. Cool slightly and pour over top of cake. Serve warm with vanilla ice cream.

Live your life so that you won't be afraid to be the first woman to leave a ladies' bridge party.

169

This wonderful old ranch that has been the site of weddings and funerals and births, and holidays, and much love. I could sense it all surrounding me.

Far below, I could see the pond where Andrew first kissed me. Off to the left, the place where Louis and Meg sleep, and on the right the orchard where I love to read. The pastures and meadows spread out before me, dotted with cattle and horses. Beyond were the mountains still frosted with the slightest bit of white. And beyond that, miles and miles of freedom. I imagined that if I could see far enough to the Southeast I would see you standing there in full view of my mind's eye. I wondered what you truly looked like now after all these years - -the details photographs do not reveal. Is your hair still as red? Do you still love to dance? Are you still the imp I remember? Though my brain tells me you are fifty-nine years of age, my memory has frozen you at seventeen. A young girl waving good-bye from a train. I wondered if I would ever see you again, or would time and distance deny me your companionship, though they could never devour our friendship.

How I love you Emily. To call you my friend seems superficial somehow. I would, instead, call our link endless, like that of sisters. I miss you.

Lovingly, Hannah

Hannah's Perfect Pie Crust

Okay, let's stop being intimated by pie crust. This crust is easy to make and produces a light flaky textured pie crust every time. Using the right ingredient is the key — highest quality, pure vegetable, butter-flavored shortening. If you use the best you will create the best!

Makes dough for 2 (one top, one bottom) pie crusts

Ingredients:
2 cups flour
1 cup butter-flavored shortening
1 Tbl. sugar
1 tsp. salt
COLD water

Utensils:
large bowl
rolling pin
waxed paper
9 or 10 inch pie plate
kitchen scissors

Putting it all together:

1. Combine flour, sugar and salt.
2. Cut in shortening. (Using your hands works the best).
3. Put about half a cup of the mixture in the palm of your hand and squeeze. Mixture should just barely hold together when touched. Too moist? Add a little flour. Too dry? Add a little shortening.
4. Now start adding water a few drops at a time and GENTLY mix through flour mixture. Note: Pie crust is a tender sort. Handle with care. The less you touch it the flakier it is.
5. Keep adding water until dough will hold together enough to form two large balls of dough.

Continued next page ➡

Behind every great man stands an amazed mother-in-law.

September 8, 1944

Dear Hannah,

Franklin and I were fishing at our favorite fishing hole yesterday, the place where we like to catch bass. It was a glorious fall day. The colors shouted to us from the trees in brilliant shades of orange, yellow and rusty pink. The sun shone brightly, as we drove down the narrow road to the pond, and there was not a single cloud in the sky to dull the day. It was cool, early on but warmed up considerably by mid-day. Perfect.

We fished for awhile and then decided on a bit of lunch. We walked up the pathway to get the picnic basket from the automobile. I was in the lead, but I never saw the snake, though Franklin did. It was a huge cottonmouth and I had walked right past it. Thank goodness I was wearing my heavy boots, because that nasty snake struck at me and indeed connected with my ankle. It felt like someone had kicked me, so I whirled around to see why Franklin would do such a thing and there was the snake! It was big. (Of course this all happened in a matter of seconds though it seemed like slow motion.) I looked up at Franklin and knew he had seen the snake strike.

Well, knowing that living around poisonous snakes is something that I have never adjusted to and that I tend to get hysterical about, Franklin thought he should not alarm me. Keeping me calm if I had been bitten was his main concern.

"Emily, stand very still." I heard him say. Stand still indeed! The horrid thing was coiling up and I was going to have no part of it! I turned and began to run screaming down the path toward the road. Poor Franklin could not have known, that though the snake had struck me, my boot had protected me from the venom. He reasoned that if I was bitten I shouldn't be doing all that screaming, not to mention running.

I was screaming and waving my arms and running in absolute terror by the time Franklin caught up with me. He grabbed me and pulled me to the ground and tried to calm me as he pulled off my boot.

6. Cut 4 one foot square (approx.) pieces of waxed paper. Gently press one ball of dough between two sheets of paper and roll out dough to form circle about 1/8 inch thick and 12 inches in diameter using short shaping motions.

7. Remove top layer of wax paper and turn dough circle out into pie plate.

8. Gently shape dough to pie plate. (Lots will be draped over the sides).

9. Fill pie with favorite filling.

10. Repeat steps 6 and 7.

11. Now comes the fun part. Gently mold top crust around filling. Do this using cupped hands.

12. Trim edges of pies crusts with clean kitchen scissors to allow only 1/4 inch over-lap of dough over lip of pie plate.

13. Press edges of dough together with thumb and forefinger and fold under. Pinch crust along lip of pie plate, all the way around to seal.

14. Make several decorative cuts in top crust to let steam escape as pie cooks.

15. Now bake this baby according to individual pie instructions.

16. Oh, you did so good! Sit down, pour yourself a fresh cup of coffee and put your feet up (or you could go dancing) and give yourself a big pat on the back! (But don't break your arm).

Public Speaking is that magical time when all the moisture from your mouth goes directly to your armpits.

I was trying to tell him that I was not hurt but my hysterical behavior had pretty much worked him up too. Then suddenly he got this strange look on his face and he let go of me. He sat back on his heels and put a hand over his heart. Hannah, my breath caught in my throat as I watched him — thinking surely he was having another heart attack. But after awhile he caught his breath and I caught mine. Though nothing serious occurred, I realized how fragile our existence really is on this earth. How easily our sunny day could have turned to utter tragedy.

Tonight as we drank our coffee out on the porch swing, Franklin and I relived the events of the day. When I asked Franklin about his heart — when I told him how frightened for him I had been — I could not hold my tears back. I wondered how I would live without him if he had died. I was afraid, but he comforted me as only he can. He told me how I would survive. How I would be comfortably provided for and how I should not be afraid of the future. Why is it that he perceived my fears to be connected with my financial security and not my emotional dependence on a love that he and I have developed and nurtured since our youth.

And now today as I write this letter, I realize that all those feelings of independence I had as a young woman have somehow gone by the wayside and how my love for Franklin is so deep and encompassing that I have become lost inside it. I believe this is normal for two people who have spent all these many years together, but the fact is, we humans are mortal and we all will die someday. This strong bond between a man and a woman linked by love; does it die too? Perhaps my fears yesterday when I thought Franklin might die, were for myself and not for him. —fear of my life without him, rather than the loss of his life. A selfish fear? Someday when one of us dies will the one left behind mourn for the other — or for themselves?

I hope I have not made you sad discussing this. Forgive me if I have. Who else could I confide my feelings to? It is you that I trust.

With love, Emily

Mom's Hot Apple Pie

An American tradition.
<u>Makes one 9-10 inch pie</u>

Ingredients:
8 large tart apples peeled and thick sliced
2 cups sugar
2 Tbl. butter

2 Tbl. flour
1 cup water

1 cup apple sauce
2 tsp. cinnamon
1 tsp. nutmeg
1/2 tsp. allspice
Utensils:
lg. pot
9-10 inch pie plate
rolling pin

Putting it all together:

1. Put the apples, butter and half the water in covered pot and simmer over low heat until apples are about half cooked. (Apples are pre-cooked to avoid shrinkage during baking, giving your pie a "Grand Canyon" effect!)
2. In covered jar shake together flour and remaining water. Pour over apples and toss to mix. Add sugar and stir gently. Add remaining ingredients and stir again.
3. When liquid thickens, remove from heat and set aside to cool slightly while you make the crust. 4. Follow the directions for **Hannah's Perfect Pie Crust** on pages 171 and 173.
5. Fill pie crust and brush top of pie with milk, then sprinkle with sugar before baking. Bake at 425 degrees for 10 minutes. Reduce heat and continue baking at 350 degrees for 45 minutes or until pie is golden brown, bubbles, and smells like apple pie.
6. Cool and slice. (My husband, Jack, likes his pie slathered with ice cream, but I have a friend that wants a slice of cheddar cheese melted on top. I like mine plain. How about you?)

A tea kettle is an amazing appliance.
After all, I'd love to see you sing with your
nose full of boiling water!

June 5, 1945

Dear Emily,

Hurrah! Hurrah! The war is over! I realize that this will be no great news by the time you receive this letter. It's over, Em. It's really over and I still find myself dancing a little jig at the mere thought. It's over, Em. Nobody else has to die. No more bombs and madmen. No more, no more, no more! Andrew agrees with President Truman, that this will, finally, be the war to end all wars. I hope both of these great men are right.

Nothing else to say. I just wanted you to share in my happiness today.

Love,

Hannah

176

Montana Huckleberry Pie

Oh yeah! Not too sweet or too tart.
Makes one 10 inch pie

Ingredients:
3 cups fresh or frozen
huckleberries or blueberries
1 cup sugar (3/4 for blueberry)
1/2 cup flour
8 oz. whipping cream

dash nutmeg
1 Tbl. butter

Utensils:
9-10 inch pie plate
rolling pin

Putting it all together:

1.   Follow the directions for **Hannah's Perfect Pie Crust** on pages 171 and 173.
2.   Toss berries with flour, sugar, and nutmeg.
4.   Spoon into pie crust.
5.   Cover with cream and drop butter on top.
6.   Brush top of pie with milk, then sprinkle with sugar before baking. Bake at 425 degrees for 10 minutes. Reduce heat and continue baking at 350 degrees for 45 minutes or until pie is golden brown, begins to bubble. Do not over cook this pie — cream may curdle.
7.   Let cool and then chill it to make sure pie "sets up" thoroughly.
8.   Ice cream? Yes ma'am.

The best way to wake up with a smile on your face is to sleep with a coat hanger in your mouth.

August 16, 1945

Dear Hannah,

It seemed like I had watched this scene before, and then I realized I had. All those young men pouring from ships into the arms of waiting loved ones.

Amanda searched the decks for Mitchell and when she saw him, Franklin and I stood with the twins and watched as Amanda hurried through the crowd, determined to get to Mitchell. Spencer and Nicholas had not seen their father in nearly three years and they were hesitant, not sure they would remember him.

It seemed like such a long time since Mitchell had been home, and though Amanda, in her typical head strong fashion, had managed to keep their business running all alone, it had been a struggle.

I saw Mitchell grab her and whirl her around and then kiss her deeply, oblivious to the crowd. And then we were all together hugging and crying and talking all at once. Relief washed over me, and fear washed from me, and I was reminded of what you said, several months ago. "No more! No more! No more!"

All my love, Em

Franklin's Favorite Mincemeat Pie

An absolute explosions of tastes to savor!

Note; You can make this with prepared mincemeat or use the recipe for Vension mincemeat on page 123 — No vension? This recipe works great with beef too!

Makes one 9- 10 inch pie

Ingredients:
2 cups mincemeat
1 cup applesauce
1 cup raisins
2 Tbl. rum
1 egg

Utensils:
large bowl
9-10 inch pie plate

Putting it all together:

1. Follow the directions for **Hannah's Perfect Pie Crust** on pages 171 and 173.
2. Mix together all the ingredients.
3. Fill pie crust.
4. Brush top of pie with milk, then sprinkle with sugar before baking. Bake at 425 degrees for 10 minutes. Reduce heat and continue baking at 350 degrees for 45 minutes or until pie is golden brown and begins to bubble.
5. Cool and slice.
Note: This pie is great with hazelnut coffee topped with whipping cream.

Chaos is six women plus one luncheon check.

June 22, 1946

Dear Emily,

Thank you for your letter, Em. Yes, my dear, I will be all right. I am in good hands, though it is only today that I am able to write to you of my grief.

I could not believe what I was seeing. I was walking to the garden to do some weeding when I heard that sickening noise. I knew immediately what it was but refused to believe it. But when I looked up I could see the tractor on its side out in the field the engine still straining. I knew what I would find before I ever reached him. How could this have happened? My poor darling Andrew. My only hope is that God took him quickly, and that he didn't suffer. I have often asked how much more am I to endure?

I awakened this morning at 4:30. The sun was just rising and I leaned against the window, pressing my forehead to the glass. I wanted to cry, but couldn't. Then all of a sudden I was angry, so very angry, Em! "Lord, why Andrew? Why have you done this to me," I screamed.

I was filled with hurt and anger as I trudged through the mornings chores, cursing the pain that consumed me beyond what I thought I could ever bear. My faithful Liddy stood in her stall patiently waiting, ready to do her job of filling my empty bucket with milk. I sat down on the milk stool that Andrew had made for me years before. And then the tears came. I wept for Andrew and A. J. and Abby and myself. I leaned my face against Liddy's huge belly and let my grief and rage wash over me in a rush of self pity. My precious old milk cow stood quietly and let me pour out my agony. And then it was over. A peace had filled me — an indescribable peace, Emily. It was like the peace I felt when I said good-bye to Papa that day. I knew at that moment, as I will for the rest of my life that I am but a small part of a big plan and that all things happen in their own time. We go through life taking so much for granted, all wrapped up in the tedium of day to day living. And then everything changes without warning. Oh, Emily, there

Chocolate-Mint Mousse Pie

Smoother than smooth.
Makes 9-10 inch pie

Ingredients:
The Crust:
2 cups graham cracker crumbs
1/2 cup brown sugar
1/2 cup butter melted
The Filling:
4 oz. semi-sweet chocolate
1/3 cup milk
2 Tbl. sugar
4 oz. cream cheese
10 finely crushed peppermint candies
5 broken (lightly crushed)
peppermint candies
2 Tbl. grated chocolate
The Topping:
1 cup whipping cream
whipped with:
2 Tbl. powdered sugar
1 drop peppermint extract

Utensils:
mixing bowl and mixer
9-10 inch pie plate
small sauce pan

Putting it all together:

1. Mix all the ingredients for crust in bowl, then press into pie plate and bake at 300 degrees for 5 to 8 minutes. Cool completely.
2. Heat chocolate and 2 Tbl. of the milk. Stir until chocolate melts.
3. Beat sugar into cream cheese. Add remaining milk and chocolate mixture and beat until smooth.

4. Fold in <u>finely</u> crushed candies.
5. Fill crust and top with whipping cream. Sprinkle with remaining crushed peppermint candies and grated chocolate.

What this country really needs is a shopping cart with wheels that all go in the same direction.

was so much I didn't say to Andrew. I wondered, did he know that I loved him more than life itself? Did he know that he filled my life with joy and meaning? Did he know that half of me was him? Of course he did.

Emily, death is a part of living and you cannot have one without the other. From this loss I will eventually heal.

You asked me once if the love between a man and a woman dies along with the body. It does not. I feel still strangely connected to Andrew and it is not a disquieting feeling — more like a presence of memories that could never leave me.

Love, Hannah

Luscious Lemon Meringue Pie

This was my father's favorite and I have the fondest memories of my mother baking this pie for Sunday dinners.
<u>Makes 9-10 inch pie</u>

Ingredients:

The Filling:
1 1/2 cups sugar
2 cups water
1/2 tsp. salt
1/2 cup cornstarch
4 egg yolks beaten
(Don't forget to save the whites for the meringue)
1/2 cup fresh lemon juice

3 Tbl. butter
9-10 inch pre-bake pie shell
The Meringue:
4 egg whites (room temp.)
1/2 tsp. cream of tartar
1/2 cup sugar
Utensils:
medium sauce pan
9-10-inch pie plate
mixing bowl and mixer

Putting it all together:

2. Pre-bake crust until barely done. (Don't forget to riddle it with fork holes before baking to keep crust from bubbling.)
3. In sauce pan, combine first four ingredients and cook over low heat, stirring constantly. Cook until thick and clear and remove from heat.
4. Combine egg yolks and lemon juice and stir into thickened mixture. Return to heat and cook again until mixture bubbles. Stir in butter. Cool, covered, for 10 minutes. Pour into pie shell, cover with plastic wrap and chill.
6. 30 minutes before serving, pre-heat oven to 375 degrees.
7. Beat egg whites, in clean metal or glass mixing bowl at highest speed, with cream of tartar, until white and fluffy. Gradually add sugar 1 Tbl. at a time, and whip meringue until stiff. Pile onto pie making sharp peaks with spoon. Watching carefully to not burn the meringue, bake until golden. Cut and serve immediately. Store remainder (ha! ha!) of pie in refrigerator.

Her: "Why don't you nibble on my neck the way you used too, honey?"
Him: "Okay, go get my teeth."

183

October 8, 1946

Dear Hannah,

My darling Hannah, I have cried many bitter tears over your loss in the past few months; feeling your hurts; sharing your pain. I am consoled that you will weather all this pain, and I know you will carry on in your strong willed fashion, but I fear you will not allow yourself to mourn. I fear you will bury your emotions in that deep pit you call survival. It is all right to miss him, Hannah. It is okay to push forward, but it is all right to miss him.

By the way my dear friend, I always knew you were quite mad, but this time I am sure you have totally lost your mind. Tell me it isn't true! You have sold the ranch and opened a pastry shop in town! Hannah, how could you? What do you know about running a business? Contrary to popular belief, Hannah, you are not 20 years of age any more! Didn't anyone bother to tell you that you are an old lady? Doing business and showing a profit do not easily go hand in hand. Honestly, Hannah, what next?

I will admit that you have always been a wizard in the kitchen and that you can squeeze a penny into submission better than anyone I know, but a pastry shop? Well at least you sound happy, which is an unimaginable relief since Andrew's death. In fact you sound more than happy. You sound enthusiastic, energetic and ambitious! Don't tell me you are actually having fun at this?

I really worried that Andrew's death would be the end of you, too. I should have learned not to underestimate you a long time ago.

Well, my dear. Good luck and best wishes to your "Huckleberry Hannah's Homemade Pastries". I am hoping you will be a tremendous success! You exhaust me!

Love, Em

Sweet Dreams Strawberry Pie

Light as a cloud and just as beautiful.

Makes 9-10 inch pie

Ingredients:
The Crust:
1 1/2 cup graham crackers crushed
1/2 cup ginger snaps crushed
1 tsp. cinnamon
1/2 cup melted butter
The Filling:
1-2 cups fresh whole strawberries (or raspberries work good too.)
1 cup sliced strawberries
2 cups mashed strawberries
1 cup sugar

4 Tbl. cornstarch
The Topping:
1 cup marshmallow creme
1 cup whipping cream whipped with 1/2 cup sugar and 1 tsp. vanilla
1/2 cup sour cream whisked with 1/2 cup sugar
dash of nutmeg
Utensils:
medium bowl
mixer and mixing bowl
9-10 inch pie plate
medium sauce pan

Putting it all together:
1. Mix crust ingredients together and press into pie plate. Bake at 300 degrees for 5 minutes. Cool and chill.
2. Line crust bottom with whole berries. (Use as many as crust will hold and mash the rest for sauce.)
3. In sauce pan, combine sugar, cornstarch and stir in mashed berries. Bring to boil and cook 3 minutes.
4. Pour over whole berries and chill 30 minutes.
5. Fold together marshmallow creme, whipped cream and sour cream.
3. Pile on pie, place sliced berries decoratively in topping and chill until set. Yum!

The only one who still pays with cash, is the Tooth Fairy.

March 22, 1947
Dear Emily,
        I said goodbye to this old place today.
So many memories here at Calliope Spring,
but I am drawn to begin anew. Clare and
Robert nearly decided to take it over, but it
simply was not meant to be, and in the end, I sold the ranch to a
young couple I hope will love it, and cause it to flourish.

        I walked out to the family cemetery, Em and said good-
bye to Andrew. I remembered him standing there tearless as his
father was buried, and strong when we laid Meg to rest. I
suppose I never thought about him lying here. I suppose I never
let my mind suggest that we would ever be parted. Foolish.
Death is a part of life, a lesson I have learned time and time
again. I just never thought I would lose Andrew.

        Tomorrow I will be in a new home, starting a new life,
living a new dream, and though I have wept over the change, I
am ready to go. I promise to be strong.

        Oh, Em. Don't worry about me. You know I had to
sell the ranch. Who would work it? All the children are gone
and have their own lives. I offered it to Patrick, but you know
Pat, he's no rancher. His interests are in medicine and I'm
glad he could not be persuaded to change. So the only sensible
thing to do was sell. Of course it wasn't easy! I raised seven
children on that ranch — not to mention myself. But everything
has its purpose, and everyone has their day. I was able to walk
away with no regrets, taking with me many happy memories.
Now it's time for something new.

        Emily, it's been a big adjustment. Living in town is
something I have never done, and small town gossip drives me
absolutely mad, but I'm getting used to it. I get out of bed
every day with a smile on my face and purpose in my heart. I
am sixty-three years old and I am not getting any younger, so I
have to make every day count. That is why I decided to open the
pastry shop. Huckleberry Hannah's Homemade Pastries was
just the ticket to make me tick. I love it.

        It's just the cutest little shop. Only 8 tables with blue

Very Berry Dessert Sauce

Both of these sauces are terrific over ice cream, pound cake, fresh fruit— whatever is in your imagination.

Ingredients
2 cups frozen berries (huckleberries, raspberries, strawberries, blackberries, boysenberries, gooseberries. Need I go on?)
juice of one lemon
1/2 cup sugar
1/2 tsp. cornstarch
1/4 cup Grand Mariner liqueur

Putting it together:
1. Combine fruit and lemon juice in blender and puree. Strain to remove seeds.

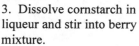

2. In sauce pan, bring to boil berry mixture and sugar. Simmer 5 minutes.

3. Dissolve cornstarch in liqueur and stir into berry mixture.

4. Remove from heat and cool. Store covered in refrigerator.

Hot Fudge Sauce

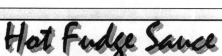

Ingredients:
3 oz. unsweetened chocolate
1/2 cup butter
1 1/2 cups sugar
1/2 tsp. salt
3/4 cup evaporated milk
1/2 tsp. vanilla

Putting it together:
Heat ingredients all together in a heavy sauce pan and bring to a rolling boil. Remove from heat and cool. Pour into covered container and store in refrigerator.

Note: The sauce is thin to make *you* thick.

When your ship finally comes in, you will usually find relatives waiting on the dock.

and white checked table cloths and white dishes decorated with tiny blue cornflowers. I write the menu on a big black board. The soup of the day is whatever I feel like making, and the pastries are made fresh every morning. I have a big kitchen to stir around in, and a front porch with a swing just so I can think of you when I have a few spare moments. That front porch is a pretty popular place! I get lots of company. All the old fogies, like me, come around about 10:00 in the morning for coffee and a sugar puff or a Danish roll. Then at noon I get all the "regulars" for soup and sandwich. And at 3:00 the school kids come by to visit, have a soda, and gobble up all the broken cookies that I can't sell. (I have been known to break a few extra cookies around 2:30 just so I don't run out.) I usually close the shop around 5:00, but nobody seems to notice, and almost every evening I will have a few folks looking for a quiet place to sip a little tea and chew a little fat. And everybody under the age of thirty calls me "Grandma"!

This will surprise you, Em. The shop is actually in Aunt Augusta and Uncle Justin's old newspaper office and I have the entire upper floor living space to myself. It is warm and sunny and really quite roomy as you surely must remember. More than enough space for one old lady and I am comforted with memories of Abby, Grandpa and of course, Aunt Augusta and Uncle Justin. The other night I stood at the window — the same place I stood the night before my wedding when I was having second thoughts about marrying. I stood there and could almost feel Andrew and the great love he lavished on me all those years. Be assured that true love never dies, Em. It comforts me.

I have adopted a fat, lazy calico cat — or she adopted me — that I named Whimsy. A real character that cat. During the day she lounges on the porch and tries to act bored with all the goings on. She never pays any attention to anyone "adult", but around 2:00 in the afternoon she perches herself on the porch railing and waits for the children to stop by. What a funny little creature. I enjoy her and she is good company.

So you see, my dear sweet Emily, I am just fine. Granted there are times late at night that I reach for Andrew in my sleep

Emily's Christmas Sugar Cookies

These are a tradition at our house.
Makes 4 dozen cut cookies

Ingredients:
2 1/4 cups flour
1/4 tsp. salt
3/4 cup sugar
1 1/2 sticks butter
1 large egg
2 tsp. almond extract
1 tsp. vanilla extract
The Frosting:
2 cups powdered sugar

1 tsp. almond extract
1 drop green or red food
coloring (will make pale green
and pink frosting)
1-5 drops cream

Utensils
lg. mixing bowl and mixer
cookie sheets
rolling pin

Putting it together:

1. Whip butter, egg, sugar, salt and extracts.
2. Gradually add flour. (This mixture may get too heavy for your mixer. Elbow grease may be needed.)
3. Cover dough and refrigerate for 2 hours.
To roll out and cut cookies:
1. Get out your favorite cookie cutters and flour.
2. Divide dough in half & roll out onto floured board to 1/4 inch thick. Cut cookies and place on greased cookie sheet.
3. Bake 5 minutes until cookies puff slightly <u>but do not brown.</u>
4. Remove from pan onto counter and cool. Frost?
5. Mix frosting ingredients together (This is a feel kind of thing). Add enough cream to make a workable, but not thin, consistency. Frost cookies and decorate with candy sprinkles, raisins, whatever. Old and young will call them winners!

*If it's such a small world,
how come it costs so much to run it.*

and remember with a pain in my heart that he isn't there any more. And there are times when I wish there was someone to talk to first thing in the morning, but all in all, I'm happy.

Clare and Robert come by nearly every Sunday and spend the day. Mary Ella and Stewart are in town twice a month, at least, and they always stay overnight with me. We laugh and stay up too late telling hilarious stories on each other and all other innocent, defenseless victims who happen to deserve to be picked on. Then of course, all the grandchildren end up here, at one time or another, in the "after school broken cookie bunch."

My life is full, Em. Praise the Lord. And when I have a weak or teary moment he is right there to take my hand and help me through it.

So don't worry. You are right about one thing though, Em. I am a terrible bookkeeper.

My love to all.
"Huckleberry Hannah" (a.k.a. "grandma")

Hannah's Chocolate Chip Slab

Just like the cookie but without the fuss.

Makes 36

1 tsp. salt
1 egg
2 cups flour
1 cup chocolate chips
1 cup chopped walnuts
(optional)

Utensils
10X15 cookie sheet with sides
mixing bowl and mixer
comfortable shoes for the cook
to work in

Ingredients
1/2 cup butter
1/2 cup butter-flavored
shortening
1 cup brown sugar
1 tsp. vanilla

Putting it together:

1. Cream first six ingredients. (Beating thoroughly is the secret).
2. Add flour gradually.
3. Stir in chocolate chips and nuts. Press mixture into cookie sheet.
4. Bake 350 degrees for 25 minutes or until center sets. Cool 5 minutes, but cut while still warm.
5. Store in covered container when cool.

*Speak well of your enemies—
remember, you made them.*

June 9, 1947
Dear Hannah,

Franklin slipped away quietly in his sleep yesterday morning. It happened just the way he wanted it to. I came in to bring his breakfast and knew he was gone. I sat next to him and held his hand for a few minutes. No tears — I shed those years ago when I knew I would lose him. So this morning, with the sun filtering in onto his peaceful face, the only thing I could say was "God's speed, my love, God's speed."

Last night I sat in the swing and rocked in the moonlight. All the years of Franklin filled me. Years of laughter and music, family and friends, babies, Christmas trees and Thanksgiving dinners surrounded me. I felt so close to him; for a moment, I almost thought I heard him whistling. Isn't that funny? The very thing that annoyed me the most for so many years is what I miss. I thought about my childhood. My wonderful childhood. I thought about you and me and all the things we have shared over the years.

Hannah, I want to come home. There is nothing left for me here, since Amanda and Mitchell moved to California, and suddenly I can't bear to be away from you and Montana one minute longer. I want to come home.

Anyway, Hannah. I was thinking. You are alone. I am alone. Why don't we be two old widows alone together? I could be a big help, you know. After all I'm sure you could use someone with a good head for business right about now.

Write me and tell me what you think of my idea. We belong together now.

Loving you, Emily

P.S. Maybe we could call the shop Hannah's Homemade Pastries and Emily's English Tea Room?

Tempting Truffle Candies

My favorite candies for your sweet tooth.

Ingredients
2/3 cup whipping cream
3 Tbl. butter
1 Tbl. sugar
2 Tbl. cornstarch
6 squares semi-sweet
chocolate chopped
2 Tbl. Amaretto (Or which-
ever liqueur you like best).
2-4 cups melted "dipping"
(tempered) chocolate
1 cup cornstarch for coating

Utensils
2 medium sauce pans
waxed paper
good music on the stereo for
working

Putting it together:
1. In sauce pan, over low heat,
combine cream, cornstarch,
butter, and sugar. Stir until
mixture is melted and begins
to bubble.
2. Remove from heat and stir
in chocolate and liqueur until
melted and well blended.
3. Refrigerate, covered for 1
hour, stirring often. (Don't
panic. This stuff is going to
look really awful for awhile,
but be patient. Mixture will
come together as it chills and
you stir.)
4. When chilled, spoon out
teaspoon sized globs and roll
into balls. Roll in cornstarch,
brushing off excess, and dip in
chocolate one at a time.
5. Place truffles on waxed
paper to cool.

**Tempering Chocolate: You
will need a candy therm-
ometer.**

1. Heat
chocolate
in double
boiler to
120
degrees.
2. Cool
to 96
degrees.
3. Dip!

*Anybody who can swallow an asprin
at a drinking fountain deserves to get well.*

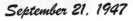

September 21, 1947

Dear Emily,

Bless your dear old heart! Of course you can come home! You're right, we do need each other and indeed we have always been a great team. "Emily's English Tea Room" is a bit much, but we can work that out when you get here. A better name might be "The Aging Filly"!

Oh, Em, if you hurry you can be home for the holidays, and I promise a white Christmas made to order just for you. We can go out caroling on Christmas Eve just like we did when we were kids. We can make popcorn and cranberry strings for the tree. And we can sit around and lie about our ages all you want. In the spring we can fish out at Sutter's Pond and Clarence Lake. Do you remember the fun we had? And pick hucklberries! And have purple fingers and tongues. And laugh, yes and laugh!

So hurry up and pack up! I can't believe you are really coming home at last.

Emily! I just had a terrible thought! What if we can't recognize each other at the train station. I'm not even going to try and described myself. I'll tell you what. Just step off that train and look for a chubby, gray haired, old lady gliding across the platform with a yellow rose in her teeth!

Hurry!

I love you, Hannah

194

Peanut Butter Creams & Creamy Peppermint Drops

These two candies are the creamiest ever.

Peanut Butter Creams

Ingredients:
4 cups powdered sugar
1 1/2 cups peanut Butter
1/3 cup milk
1/4 cup honey
1/2 tsp. salt
1 tsp. vanilla
6 oz. semi-sweet chocolate melted

Utensils
mixing bowl
medium sauce pan
9 inch sqaure pan

Putting it together:
1. Knead together first six ingredients until smooth and pat into 9 inch square pan.
2. Pour chocolate over top and cool 5 minutes, but cut into squares while still warm.
3. Store in covered container.

That's all folks.

Creamy Peppermint Drops

Ingredients:
4 oz. cream cheese
3 drops peppermint oil
2-3 cups powdered sugar

Utensils:
mixing bowl
chilled candy molds (optional)

Putting it together:
1. Knead cream cheese, peppermint oil, and enough powdered sugar to make mixture thick and stiff.
3. Roll into teaspoon sized balls and dust with powdered sugar.
4. Press into candy molds or leave in balls and wrap them in individual waxed papers.
5. Store in freezer.

My husband and I have a magical relationship.
I ask him to do the dishes and he disappears.

EPILOGUE

Hannah and Emily's story — their life together as young women growing up together in Montana — is Chronicled in *Wishes and Fishes in Bluebird,* now available. Their story continues in *Letters from Heartsong,* due to be published in 1996.

ABOUT THE AUTHOR

Deanna Hansen-Doying and her husband, Jack, are the owners of **Huckleberry Hannah's Montana Bed & Breakfast** in Northwestern Montana at Eureka. Deanna is also the author of *__Wishes and Fishes in Bluebird__*, a Montana novel, and is working on its sequel, *__Letters from Heartsong__* (copyright), along with a set of children's books due to be published in 1997.

What's in here anyway?

Starters

Salads

Soups

Breads and Pastries

What's in here... Continued

Breakfast

Chicken, Fish and Seafood

Beef, Pork and Wild Game

More....What's in here?

Emergency Baking Substitutions

1 1/2 tsp. cornstarch = 1 Tbl. flour
1 whole egg = 2 egg yolks plus 1Tbl. water
1 cup fresh milk = 1/2 cup evaporated milk plus 1/2 cup water
OR 1 cup reconstituted nonfat dry milk plus 2 Tbl. butter
1 oz. unsweetened chocolate = 3 Tbl. cocoa plus 1 Tbl. shortening
1 cup honey = 1 1/4 cups sugar plus 1/4 cup liquid
1/2 cup oil = 1 cup applesauce OR 1/2 cup prune puree

Equivalent Measures

3 Teaspoons = 1 Tablespoon
4 Tablespoons = 1/4 cup
1 1/3 Tablespoons = 1/3 cup
8 Tablespoons = 1/2 cup
10 2/3 Tablespoons = 2/3 cup
12 tablespoons =3/4 cup
16 tablespoons = 1 cup
1/2 cup = 1 gill
2 cups = 1 pint
4 cups = 1 quart
2 pints = 1 quart
4 quarts = 1 gallon
8 quarts = 1 peck
4 pecks = 1 bushel
1 ounce liquid =2 Tbl.
10 ounces = 1 pound
32 ounces = 1 quart
8 ounces liquid = 1 cup

A Great Gift!

Please send me: _____ copies of **Huckleberry Hannah's Montana Country Sampler Cookbook.** I have enclosed **$13.95 plus $2.00 shipping and handling** per copy. Enclosed $_____. (Canadian orders: Please pay in U.S. funds and allow an additional $1.00 for shipping.)

Please send me: _____ copies of **Wishes and Fishes in Bluebird.** I have enclosed **$12.95 plus $2.00 shipping and handling** per copy. Enclosed $_____. (Canadian orders: Please pay in U.S. funds and allow an additional $1.00 for shipping.)

Make checks payable to:
Bluebird Press
P.O. Box 664
Eureka, MT 59917